CASE STUDIES TALK SHEETS &DISCUSSION STARTERS

Jim Burns and Mark Simone

GENERAL
EDITOR

COMPILER

Gospel Light

Gospel Light is an evangelical Christian publisher dedicated to serving the local church. We believe God's vision for Gospel Light is to provide church leaders with biblical, user-friendly materials that will help them evangelize, disciple and minister to children, youth and families.

We hope this Gospel Light resource will help you discover biblical truth for your own life and help you minister to youth. God bless you in your work.

For a free catalog of resources from Gospel Light please contact your Christian supplier or call 1-800-4-GOSPEL.

PUBLISHING STAFF
William T. Greig, Publisher
Dr. Elmer L. Towns, Senior Consulting Publisher
Dr. Gary S. Greig, Senior Consulting Editor
Jill Honodel, Editor
Pam Weston, Assistant Editor
Kyle Duncan, Associate Publisher
Bayard Taylor, M.Div., Editor, Theological and Biblical Issues
Debi Thayer, Designer

How to Make Clean Copies from This Book

You may make copies of portions of this book with a clean conscience if:
- you (or someone in your organization) are the original purchaser;
- you are using the copies you make for a noncommercial purpose (such as teaching or promoting your ministry) within your church or organization;
- you follow the instructions provided in this book.

However, it is ILLEGAL for you to make copies if:
- you are using the material to promote, advertise or sell a product or service other than for ministry fund-raising;
- you are using the material in or on a product for sale;
- you or your organization are **not** the original purchaser of this book.

By following these guidelines you help us keep our products affordable.
Thank you,
Gospel Light

*Pages with the following notation can be legally reproduced:

Contents

Talk Sheets ········· 32

Object Lessons ········· 55

Discussion Starters ········· 71

Storybook Ideas:
Dr. Seuss and Other Stories

Dedication

This book is dedicated to special men in my life who have guided and directed me into and along the paths of Christ. Through these examples, I have experienced God's goodness and have found wisdom for my own life.

My grandfathers: Harry Schlauch, Frank Simone, Gould Morton and John Gladish.

My fathers: Sam Simone, Herb Floyd and Jack Gladish.

My pastors: Clayton Witt, Pete Peterson, George Taylor, Don Preslan and David Norling.

My brothers: Ron Simone, Matt Simone and Jonathon Floyd.

My sons: Daniel Simone and Nicholas Simone.

My teachers: Mel Somerski, Dick Myers, Tom Koloos and Ray Steffner.

My friends: Jim Burns, Richard Whitmore, Tom Patterson, Chris Hill, Bill Britton, George McClelland, Earl Barnett, Tim Thomas, John Bondarenka, Dean Bruns, David Maske, Alif Kuri, David Palmstrom, Jim Rouru, Larry Trace and John Bourisseau.

I thank each one of you, still living or now with the Lord, for your friendship, love and investment in my life and ministry. As I share your gifts with others through my life, your legacy of love continues. And so the circle remains unbroken and the Body of Christ is built.

Mark Simone

Acknowledgments

Everyone working with a book knows that it takes many people to make the final product a reality. So many help who remain "behind the scene." Thank you all for your help and support.

However, occasionally a person emerges who is so critical to the project, so important to the face, spirit, development and outcome, that not to acknowledge and thank that person would be akin to sin.

Jill Corey, who works with Jim Burns at the National Institute of Youth Ministry, is such a person. Her calm influence, good humor, remarkable mind and quick solutions have made this process a great joy.

Thank you, Jill, for being the person God has made you to be. You are truly a great friend.

Mark Simone

Contributors

Karen Bosch is a third-grade teacher at Southfield Christian School in Michigan. For 24 years she has volunteered mega hours for Youth for Christ. A computermeister, she has designed interactive computer games.

Mike DeVries serves as youth pastor at Yorba Linda Friends Church in Orange County, California. He has served as a trainer of youth workers and has written the YouthBuilders Group Bible Study *The Word on the New Testament.* He and his wife and son life in Southern California.

Jenni Knowles is training director at Young River Ministries near Detroit and teaches future youth pastors at Williams Tyndale College. Her joyful avocation involves undertaking major home repair projects, sometimes at 2 A.M.

Tom Patterson is a pastor in California who has ministered to teenagers in the continental U.S., Alaska, Eastern Europe and the Ukraine. An avid rock climber, Tom can say "I do not like raisins" in 12 languages.

Scott Rubin is Director of Student Ministries at the Village Church in Rancho Santa Fe, California. He has been known to refer to his wife and his golden retriever in the same breath.

Mark Simone has been ministering to kids in Ohio for nearly 18 years. He is the author of *Ministering to Kids Who Don't Fit* (Accent Publications, 1993) and coauthor, with his wife Kathy, of *Teaching Today's Youth* (Accent, 1996). He wishes that one day all of the kids he has worked with would send him to Italy for a vacation.

Jonathan Traux is a youth pastor who, after four years of ministry, is just beginning to learn the lessons his teenagers are trying to teach him. He lives in Louisville, Ohio with his wife Debbie and his son Daniel.

Daiv Whaley is a writer and youth worker who works with emotionally troubled children. He resides in the beautiful hills of Akron, Ohio. He also writes short stories and articles about modern rock music.

Introduction

I hope you will love this book as much as I do! As a youth worker and the general editor of this project, I know how beneficial it is to get students talking and discussing the important issues of their lives. I think you will agree that this book has a little something for everybody in it when it comes to getting your students to open up and talk. As you are well aware, students learn best when they talk, not when we talk at them.

Edgar Dale, one of the great educators of this century, developed the Cone of Experiential Learning. His Cone informs us that when students are spoken or written to their retention level is only 5 to 10 percent, but when they are active participants in experiential learning, the retention can be expanded to as much as 85 percent. That's why this book is so important.

Mark Simone and I asked youth workers from the front lines to send us their best stuff for getting students to think and talk about the important real-life issues of living out their Christianity. In this book you will find case studies taken directly out of real situations and other types of discussion starters that have already been used successfully with students. You'll be introduced to a wonderful style of teaching and learning that encourages thought-provoking discussions.

Our goal as Christian youth workers and teachers of adolescents is to plant God's Word in students' lives and to help them actively live out their faith. Oftentimes using the kinds of experiences in this book will do a better and more effective job than any sermon or youth talk. A discussion in which the students discover the truth for themselves with your guidance becomes a very powerful tool for active learning. In this book you will find useful tools for active learning in this resource.

God bless you as you help youth navigate through the not-so-easy world of adolescence. Thanks for being a difference-maker and for being committed to youth.

Jim Burns
San Clemente, California

Case Studies

As a youth leader, you know the importance of making a lesson relevant and familiar to the experiences of young people. A lesson with a point that is taken from the youth experiences of the 1970s may be lost on your listeners because they have not shared the experience. If teenagers can't relate, they will assume that the point is not for them. An effective way to personalize a lesson is to use a case study that reflects the realities of today's youth.

Case studies use people's real-life experiences that have a common point for all of humanity. With little effort we can either relate to what has happened or picture ourselves within the situation. A case study goes deeper than an illustration by drawing us into the situation and asking us to face our own likely reactions even though we are not in reality involved. Learning occurs at a deeper level when we imagine how we would react or respond in a similar situation.

The following case studies include ques-

tions to help you personalize the topics by encouraging the listener to explore how he or she would face the problems.

These case studies can stand on their own for use as short single-topic lessons. Use them for conversations during seemingly endless bus trips. Spring one on the group at a campfire. Or you can incorporate one into an evening meeting topic or a Sunday School lesson.

It is important that the case study be adapted to fit who you are. Make it seem natural. Be clear on the details of the story. Be conversational. Don't answer every question—allow the teenagers some space and time to grapple with their personal responses.

The studies enclosed are true stories, but some details have been changed to keep the participants anonymous. At the end of each study suggested topics are listed to help you in selecting an appropriate study for your desired lesson.

The Mission Trip

The youth group of First Church boarded the plane for Alaska for the most ambitious cross-cultural mission trip they'd ever planned. The two weeks they would spend in a remote Native Alaskan village doing evangelism and helping the local pastor repair the church's deteriorating facilities had taken an enormous amount of planning, prayer and training on the part of the students and the adult leaders. The excitement level was high as the plane lifted off, and it remained high the following day as they boarded smaller bush planes that brought them to their final destination.

On the group's first night in the village, four residents approached a number of the students who were relaxing outside the church building. They asked them why they had come to the village. The students explained who they were and what they hoped to accomplish while they were there. They invited the villagers to come to the evangelistic services that they would be leading later in the week.

The four residents were frankly unimpressed and declined their invitation. They told the student missionaries that from their perspective, the Christian church had played the major role in destroying their culture, their language, their art and their sense of identity as Alaskan native people. They went on to detail for the students how this had come about and even suggested they should leave the village earlier than they'd planned.

Later that evening, the youth group members discussed whether or not it was appropriate for them to be sharing their faith in a culture they apparently knew little about.

Discussion Questions

1. How would you summarize the situation facing the student missionaries?

2. Were the village residents being fair in their critique of the Christian church? Explain your answer.

3. Are all things done with sincerity "in the name of Christ" appropriate? Why or why not?

4. Are there some cultures which should be left alone by Christians? Why or why not?

5. If you were a leader of the youth group, what would you have said to the students?

Possible Topics

Cross-cultural missions, racial issues, mission trips, evangelism

Is He the Only Way?

The youth pastor had just finished delivering his talk on the uniqueness of Jesus Christ, based on John 14:6, "Jesus answered, 'I am the way and the truth and the life. No one comes to the Father except through me.'" Feeling good about the depth and delivery of his talk, he dismissed the youth group for the evening with an encouraging word.

A small group of students, however, remained seated on the floor with expressions of concern on their faces. They looked nervously at one another to see who would speak for the group. Finally, one of the girls spoke up.

"We have trouble accepting some of the stuff you said tonight," she blurted out. "You said that Jesus is the only way to God and to salvation, but we think you're being too narrow-minded. Why do you think He is the only way? What's to say that Hindus or Buddhists or Muslims aren't the ones who really are tuned in to God? For that matter, how do you know that they're not *all* right in their own way? Don't you think it's kind of arrogant to say that Christians have cornered the market on truth? Besides, maybe the only reason we're Christians in the first place is because we were born in a country where Christianity is the main religion."

The other students were nodding in agreement as they looked at the youth pastor with expressions that seemed to say, "Well?"

Discussion Questions

1. Have you ever had the same questions that this group of students asked?

2. Is it possible for all religions to be true or equally valid? Why or why not?

3. What influence does a person's culture have on what religion he or she will adopt?

4. Read John 14:6. What conclusions about other religions can you draw from what Jesus said?

5. Is Jesus narrow-minded? Explain your answer.

Possible Topics

Salvation, world religions, Christ is the *only* way to God, truth

What Is Reality?

Having just attended a high school small group series on "The Life of Jesus," Kim was eager to share what she'd learned with her friends at school—particularly with those who were not Christians. In the lunch room one afternoon, she enthusiastically shared what she had learned with Josh. Josh was very attentive to her as she spoke and seemed genuinely excited about everything she had to say.

"That's so cool," he said with genuine sincerity.

Surprised, Kim asked, "Josh, are you a Christian?"

"Not really," he replied. "The Christian thing doesn't really work for me, but I think it's totally cool that it works for you."

Kim thought for a moment and said, "Well, if the Christian thing doesn't work for you, how come you're excited about it for me?"

Josh considered her question and said, "Because even though Christianity is not my reality, I wouldn't want to put you down because it's yours. Everyone's reality is different and none is better or worse than any other."

The bell for the next period rang, signaling an end to lunch and the conversation with Josh. Kim walked away wondering about some of the things he'd said.

 ## Discussion Questions

1. Have you ever had a conversation like this—from either Kim's or Josh's position? What happened?

2. How would you define the word "reality"?

3. Are there different realities for different people? Why or why not?

4. How can we know what the truth is?

5. Read Romans 1:18-23; 1 Corinthians 1:18-25; and Ephesians 4:17-24. According to Paul, how can believers clearly determine truth from error?
   What would Paul say to Kim? What would he say to Josh?

Possible Topics

Relativism, absolute truth, New Age philosophies, evangelism, disagreement, conflict

I Am a Christian

Tony found it unbelievable when he heard that Tom had been beaten in a drug deal and was almost killed. In middle school they had been best friends. When Tony became a Christian, he and Tom had drifted apart. Tom's mother had called and asked Tony to visit Tom and try to help him.

When Tony entered the room, he did not recognize his friend. Tom's face showed the results of a severe beating. He had multiple stitches and bruises, as well as swelling and flecks of dried blood. Through puffed lips Tom greeted Tony.

As the conversation proceeded, Tom told Tony about his growing drug use, his dance with crime, his downward spiral into dealing drugs and finally, what he had done to receive such a beating. Tony was absolutely shocked at what his old pal was telling him. They had grown up together, gone to Sunday School and junior high youth club. He thought he had known Tom at one time.

"Tom," Tony asked, "What happened to you that you fell so far from being a Christian?"

"I'm still a Christian, Tony," Tom explained. "I was born a Christian. I was raised a Christian. What makes you think I'm not?"

Discussion Questions

1. How would you answer Tom's question?

2. What should Tony do to let Tom see God's love for him?

3. Why might Tom believe that he is a Christian by virtue of his family background?

4. What follow-up might Tony consider in relation to Tom?

5. Read John 3:1-21 and discuss how Jesus suggested to Nicodemus that we become Christian. What is the plan?

Possible Topics

Salvation, assurance of salvation

The Missing Mugs

Melissa was only too happy to assist her father in inventorying their restaurant before the new owners took over. The sale of the family business meant that they would spend more time together and Mom had made such a great deal on the sale that it would insure Melissa's and her sister's chances to attend college.

Working alone in the basement, Melissa came across some wonderful mugs. They were handmade and glazed with a beautiful swirling decoration in her favorite shade of blue. Melissa pictured the mugs on her bookshelf at college and found them irresistible. Besides, she reasoned, the new owners would not need them since they were not really used in the restaurant. Wrapping each one carefully in newspaper, she slipped the mugs into her backpack and finished her tasks.

A few weeks later her father grumbled candidly to the whole family at the dinner table that his restaurant staff had ripped him off and how hurt he felt. After all, he had been fair to them and generous in his wages. He had openly allowed his Christian values to guide him in his dealings with his employees and now they had robbed him.

Tammy, the youngest daughter, asked what had been stolen.

He said, "A set of mugs that were made for me by my old army buddy. He gave them to me just before he died. It is the only thing that I have to remember him by and now they are gone."

The rest of the meal was eaten in silence.

In her room Melissa cried into her pillow. What should she do? She did not know that the mugs were her father's. He would never suspect that she took them. How could she be so stupid, hurting her dad in the process?

Discussion Questions

1. What would you do if you were in Melissa's shoes?

2. Did she actually steal the mugs or is it just a misunderstanding?

3. What might happen if Melissa just kept quiet about the missing mugs?

4. How might this event harm Melissa's relationship with her dad?

5. How might this be resolved?

Possible Topics

Honesty, misunderstanding, making wrongs right, confession, stealing, rationalizing, consequences of actions, repentance

The Campus Confrontation

The youth group of First Church often linked up with the college campus group at State University for fun activities. Pastor Eric was the leader of both groups so the occasional united meetings made sense.

On one occasion the whole group was eating in the outdoor campus commons area when a traveling preacher called Brother Ned began addressing people in the commons in a loud voice. He preached a sermon first to nobody, and then to the large crowd that began to gather.

In his remarks, Ned called cheerleaders and girls wearing jeans "whores and harlots of Satan." He referred to other nationalities as "animals and pagans who intend to dissolve the blood of the white man." Higher education was called "the nonsense of the liberals." The longer he spoke, the nastier and more agitated the crowd became. Students began spitting on Ned, calling him equally foul names and throwing soft drinks at him.

Suddenly, one student ran to the table where Pastor Eric and the mixed group of high school and college students were sitting and screamed at them, "You're Christians! How can you just sit there and not do something? Do you support what this nut is saying?" Then he walked away in disgust.

Discussion Questions

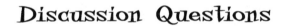

1. What do you think of Brother Ned's point of view?

2. What about the angry accusation of the student?

3. What would you have done in this situation?

4. What could Pastor Eric and the students do to counteract Ned's speech?

5. Which group's behavior was worse—Ned's or those who spit, hit and screamed at him?

Possible Topics

Unchristlike Christianity, intolerance, prejudice, racism, sexism, the gospel of hatred, taking a stand

Can Dish It Out, but Can't Take It

The youth at church camp were engaging in the most anticipated event of the week—the Big Game. As usual, the counselors had come up with a great group game and things were going very well. The campers were having a fabulous time in the highly active contest.

One of the counselors made a deal with a rival cabin's team that he would submit to a cream pie in the face if his team lost. This challenge only heightened the fun and made the game more intense. To the delight of the counselor, it looked like he was going to avoid the consequence of the challenge.

With victory all but assured, the counselor lightheartedly tormented his opponents with whipped cream, shaving cream and other messy gunk. Everyone was loving it, and they were taking it as it was meant—in fun.

However, the tide changed and the counselor's team very unexpectedly lost the challenge. As the winners came after him with cream pies, he fled to his cabin and locked himself in, refusing to allow the winning team their victory celebration. The director had to break up the group awaiting the counselor as they became angry and were close to damaging camp property. Later in the day the counselor returned to the group during a presentation by a guest speaker, but the damage had been done. He had given his word and broken it, and there was nothing anyone could do to restore the spirit of camp fun.

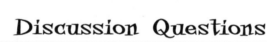

Discussion Questions

1. Why was this disappointment such a big deal to the students?

2. Did the counselor break trust? Why or why not?

3. What about the broken promise do you think bothered the teenagers the most?

4. How important is a promise made in fun?

5. How would you have handled the situation if you were...

   The counselor?

   The director of the camp?

   One of the disappointed winners?

Possible Topics

Integrity, disappointment, keeping promises, the value of your word, relationships

By Chance, Not by Choice

In a small town high school of nearly 350 students, there were only four or five students of minority races. When nonwhite visitors came to town to shop, or when a sports team with members of other races came to compete, the teens in this town were often unsure how to act. Without experiences with other races, many felt disadvantaged in relating to or understanding them.

The community was not particularly racist. It was a fairly affluent area and the fact was that in this part of the country, most minorities could not afford to live in the town or go to its schools. It was a community mostly open to others, but for economic reasons was not available to everyone.

At a youth group meeting, a leader wondered out loud how the church could promote a climate that would make other races feel comfortable. She asked if there were subtle barriers that made minorities feel discriminated against or uncomfortable. Some ideas were offered and discussed, but all seemed either too goofy or simply impossible. Finally, one student thought it might be good to contact an African-American church in a nearby community and plan a combined fun event to help both groups get to know one another.

Calls were made, but the other group was not interested and the idea fell apart. The white students felt sad and frustrated. They were white by chance, as was their community and school system, not by their choice. How could they ever bring change?

Discussion Questions

1. What might be some invisible barriers that this church or community has put up that might discourage minorities from feeling welcome?

2. How can this youth group get to know those of other races?

3. Was the African-American church being racist in declining to share in a combined event? Explain your reasoning.

4. How bad is racism in our communities, school systems and churches?

5. What barriers to racial equality does our church, school or town exhibit?

Possible Topics

Racism, reverse racism, prejudice, breaking barriers,
cross-cultural communications, perseverance

Pizza Night Divorce

It was a few years after Mark's parents divorced that a youth worker got to know him. He had been in a tailspin since the family broke up. The youth worker could see that Mark needed help badly and arranged to meet with him on a regular basis to help sort out his problems.

After a few counseling sessions, Mark tearfully admitted that he had been the cause of the divorce. It was the result of his bad decision-making and he would hold that guilt forever. Mark was sure that his parents divorced when he was in fifth grade because of something he did not do.

Gently probing, the youth worker encouraged Mark to share with him the details of how he, as a ten-year-old, could in one single situation cause something as huge as a divorce. With tears in his eyes, trembling and nearly incoherent, Mark confessed to the youth worker that his father had announced he would be leaving on Monday after Mark had missed the weekly family pizza night on Friday.

In amazement the youth worker listened as the bits of Mark's story were told to him. For years the family had eaten pizza on Friday nights prior to attending various high school sporting events. Mark's dad worked in the school's athletic department. A friend of the family invited Mark to dinner, and for the first time in his young life, he missed the family pizza gathering. Three days later, his dad left. The facts were obvious to Mark: Dad left because Mark broke tradition. The family breakup was all Mark's fault, as far as he was concerned.

Discussion Questions

1. Was the divorce Mark's fault?

2. Why would Mark believe that it was his fault?

3. What do you think really happened?

4. Have any of you believed that you were the cause of your parents' arguments or divorces?

5. Read John 8:32. How might we allow Christ to show us the truth that we might erase our erroneous beliefs?

Possible Topics

Truth, misunderstanding, personal pain, living with lies, divorce, guilt

Being the Minority

For their annual week-long work camp, the all-white youth group traveled to a Christian conference center that was frequented by nearly all African-American churches. The purpose of the experience was to share the work alongside an ethnic group that was not represented in their own community. They believed that understanding and cooperation could be fostered by tackling a project together with people they had been taught to avoid or even fear.

Their arrival coincided with an annual gathering of nearly 500 African-American Christians from a three-state area to celebrate their heritage and spirituality. Driving into the campground they saw that their 26 students were going to be the only whites among a sea of 500 blacks.

Their tasks began as soon as they climbed out of the vans. They were to assist in preparing, serving and cleaning up the lunch meal for the hundreds who were attending this one-day conference. With no introduction, they began their work.

After two hours of hard work, they gathered at empty tables to eat lunch and talk. Over delicious barbecued food, the teenagers confessed that they felt uncomfortable and ignored. They expressed concerns about their purpose for being there. Many wanted to leave immediately. A few were near tears.

Just then, a young African-American girl no more than seven years old came to their table and invited them to play catch. She was especially interested in one young woman's long, blond hair and wanted to touch it. She had never seen hair like that before. Within minutes the entire youth group was well into a game of catch.

Discussion Questions

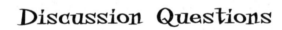

1. Why were the white students so discouraged? Were their concerns realistic?

2. How does living separately from other cultures encourage racism?

3. Why did the little girl's simple request break the ice between the two groups?

4. Have you been afraid of or uncomfortable with a different ethnic group only to find your fears had no substance?

5. Read Romans 3:22-24; 10:12,13 and Galatians 3:26-28. What is universal about these verses? How do they suggest we live?

Possible Topics

Racism, misunderstanding, the power of love, reconciliation

Assault on a Soda Machine

On a recent trip, a youth group member, Doug, had to be physically removed from the vicinity of the soda and candy machines at a gas station because he was attempting to pull them down. He was found in a flurry of kicking, hitting and shoving the machines, and the youth worker, John, had to hold his arms at his sides and pull him from the vending room of the gas station.

Outside, John asked Doug what he was doing. Doug told him that the machine took his money, giving him no change and no soda. He admitted that he had momentarily lost his temper and was intent on causing a dollar's worth of damage to the machine for ripping him off.

As he and John talked, Doug finally admitted that he was very upset because his parents had announced to the family that they were splitting up. This came on the day he was cut from the varsity basketball team, flunked a major math test and had a disagreement with his girlfriend.

Gently, John asked Doug if perhaps he was more upset about the way things were going in life than he was about losing the dollar in the machine. Doug just looked blankly at him and insisted that there was no connection.

Discussion Questions

1. What do you think was really bothering Doug?

2. How often do we take out our anger, failure or helplessness on other things or people that are not the source of our trouble?

3. Why do we react with such aggression when a small frustration ticks us off?

4. Have you ever gone nuts over a small thing? Was it a smoke screen to cover how you felt about something much more serious?

5. Read 1 Peter 5:6-11 and John 14:27; 16:33. What worries, cares or hardships are you facing alone? Would it help to share them with Jesus? Why or why not?

Possible Topics

Denial, leaning on Christ during difficulties, dealing with anger, frustration, divorce, trouble, pain

The Accident

Phil was to be one of the speakers on Youth Sunday at church. He had committed to sharing his testimony about his faith in Christ and how Jesus helped him in times of trouble and stress. It was time to start the service, the sanctuary was packed and Phil had not yet shown up.

A quick call to his house had not brought any answers either. No one had seen him. The youth group had no choice but to move on without him.

Between the first and second services the participants were enjoying donuts and juice while tweaking their parts for a better presentation when Phil walked in. It was obvious from his face that something was very, very wrong.

It had snowed all through the night and Phil was a new driver. On his way to the service he slid through a stop sign and collided with another car. He had received a few bumps and bruises, had gotten a ticket, and his car was a total loss. However, what he actually lost was far more significant.

Phil was angry with God that on the very day he was going to stand before the congregation and share about his faith, he had had this accident. He felt let down and told the other participants that he would be a hypocrite if he got up there and shared what he had written. With anger in his voice and a tear sliding down his cheek, Phil admitted that the accident had caused a great rift between him and God.

Discussion Questions

1. How would you feel if you were in Phil's shoes?

2. Was Phil being fair in his thinking? Why do bad things happen to Christians, especially when they are trying to serve God?

3. How do you think this accident will affect Phil's faith in the long run?

4. Could you have talked about your faith in God if you had been Phil? Why or why not?

5. Read Psalm 55. Have you ever felt like David and wondered where God was as you were facing tough times?

Possible Topics

Troubles, hardship, damaged faith, challenges of Christian living

The New Christian

Everyone rejoiced when Paul became a Christian. He had been the focus of prayer by many believers in the small college community for many months. Paul was a charming, wonderful young man with great friendship abilities and a generous heart. His biggest fault? He was a notorious womanizer.

Numerous times throughout any given week, Paul could be seen putting the moves on another young coed. His attractiveness was not only in his handsome looks, but he had an appealing personality. Most of the girls, even those knowing his reputation, succumbed to his allure and ended up spending the night at his apartment. Not threatened by Christians, Paul was just as friendly to believers, attracting many from the campus Christian club.

Surprising to many, Paul became a believer through a series of meaningful events and the open sharing of fellow students. Giving his first testimony, he thanked the many who had helped him and had prayed for him so diligently. He shared that he had never had any exposure to Christianity before meeting them and he thanked them for opening his eyes to the gospel.

This delightful surprise was followed by shock and despair as Paul's new sisters and brothers in Christ noted that he still continued his playboy lifestyle, dating and sleeping with as many young women as he could. The phone lines and concerned whispers buzzed with sadness and a bit too much gossip. What should be done about Paul?

Finally, after many weeks of Paul's continued philandering, one friend in Christ pulled him aside and confronted him on his sexual misbehavior. Stunned, Paul jumped to his feet, his face ablaze with embarrassment. Once calmed, he responded and said, "All of you knew that I had not been raised in the church. Christianity is very new and strange to me. Why did all of you wait so long to tell me that my behavior was wrong?"

Discussion Questions

1. Did Paul have a valid point with his question?

2. What is the responsibility of the church to new believers?

3. Have you ever had a problem with an issue of morality and been held accountable for it, even when you had no idea that you were wrong? How did you feel when confronted?

4. What should believers learn from this true story?

5. How would 1 Corinthians 6:18-20 be excellent advice for Paul?

Possible Topics

Discipling, new believers, confronting sin

Delinquents or Outcasts?

In a small affluent midwestern community, the older adults reacted with harshness and anger as the teenagers became interested in skateboarding and in-line skating. At first, they skated in empty parking lots and on streets that were not used much. After skating, they would congregate in the town square or behind some of the stores. Many adults became upset and complained to the police. After many such complaints, the police restricted skating and the accompanying loitering.

One downtown merchant became concerned that the skaters had no place to hang out. He feared that if there wasn't some space for them to use, they would resort to mischief out of boredom. He gave several of them written permission to use his private business parking lot for skating after hours. He told them to keep the permission letter with them and if questioned, simply show it to the police. He felt this would stop any problems between the teens and the officials.

One evening the skaters were stopped, questioned and finally taken into custody for violating the police order against skating. When they argued they had permission and tried to show their permission slips, the police shouted them down and refused to read the paper. They were taken to the police station and their parents were called. These so-called delinquents were all from respectable families and some were even Christians. None of them had ever caused trouble in the community before.

 ## Discussion Questions

1. How would you feel if you were one of these skaters?

2. Why might the police act this way toward these teenagers?

3. Look at both sides of the conflict. What are the legitimate concerns and needs of both the adults and the teens?

4. What better plan could be developed in communities where youth and adults clash over leisure space?

5. How might a church become involved in such a matter? Does the church have any place in community disputes such as this?

Possible Topics

Individual rights vs. community rights, the Church's influence, generational conflicts

What's in a Name?

Some of the midwestern United States youth at a work camp in Ontario, Canada immediately made friends with the local Indian youth. While hanging out during work breaks, the Indians made it clear that they were not "Native Americans." They were proud to be Indians and found the other term distasteful and offensive. Lesson one had gone well.

After a few days, Annie, a young woman from Ohio, asked her new Indian friend, "Molly, what's your Indian name?" Molly, who had obviously been asked this question many times, smiled and said, "Some days it's Sunshine. Sometimes I go with Meadow Child. But mostly I prefer to be Tall Woman Who Walks Backwards to Gather Water." Then she and her friends burst into laughter, leaving their new friends perplexed.

Later, Molly explained to all of them that so-called Indian names were not part of her tribe's modern culture. In most ways they were as current as any ethnic group. While they observed some meaningful customs and they learned traditional dances and the stories of their people, they did not pass on the ancient customs that had become irrelevant in modern society. However, her grandparents still had names that reflected nature or some identifying family characteristic.

Confused, Annie asked Molly why movies, TV and the media in general continued to portray her people in this erroneous fashion. Molly just snickered and knowingly asked Annie who she thought wrote those kinds of movies. She clarified that if the movie was a historic portrayal, it was one thing. But if it was treating an Indian like some wild, uncivilized, drunken child, it was due to Hollywood stereotyping.

Her head swimming, Annie asked one further question. "Then how can we know what to call your ethnic group? Some say you are Native Americans. You say you're an Indian. Some have symbolic names; you are simply Molly. How can we know what to call you, or any other ethnic group?" Molly said she had no clue.

But the youth pastor, Anthony, had a thought that helped. He said, "I was leading a work camp in the South and as part of our program, we had a leader of the community center talk to us about race relations. During the talk, one of the students asked him if he was black or African-American. Smiling, the man said, "My daddy was a Negro; I'm just fine with being black, but my son insists on being an African-American. The best way is to just ask us what we prefer and respect that."

 ## Discussion Questions

1. Why do we so often treat people from other cultures differently than we treat people from our own culture?

2. Was Annie being an airhead, or is her question to Molly about her Indian name one that you might have asked?

3. What did you think about Molly's treatment of Annie's question?

4. How did the answer that Anthony received about asking people what they prefer feel to you? Could you ask an ethnic person his or her preference?

5. What do you think of this issue of ethnic identity? Are you willing to walk the extra mile to insure the comfort of persons of differing culture or color? Do you think our society is becoming overly sensitive or less sensitive to the differences among us? Is it necessary to label people groups? Why or why not?

Possible Topics

Ethnic identity, cultural diversity, racial labels, understanding between races

The Invisible Homeless

The official word in Puerto Rico was that they had taken care of the homeless problem and that their country had completely achieved proper housing for all their people. But while touring San Juan, we saw a man sleeping in a doorway in an alley; his only blanket was a stained piece of cardboard.

The local newspaper in a major American city stated that the government was making great advances in resolving the problem of homelessness of that city. At the beginning of our visit, we saw very few homeless people, but by week's end we saw dozens and dozens sleeping in a park not far from the mayor's home. Our hosting pastor said that frequently the city does a mass roundup and drives the homeless out of the city into other communities. It takes about a week for them to walk back to town.

In another major city the homeless were bringing suit against the city for spending lots of money on hiding the homeless before a political convention was held in the city. The homeless argued that the huge sums of money could have been better spent on providing some kind of relief housing for them rather than rounding them up and busing them beyond the city limits or making mass arrests.

During a family vacation, a young Christian high school student got change for $50.00 and gave a dollar bill along with a word of hope and encouragement to each homeless person she saw. Her smile was reflected in the eyes of the women and men she helped in her small way. Her compassion was worth far more than any amount of money. Her parents insisted she stop this. "These people aren't homeless. They are just lazy bums. Let them get a job like the rest of us decent people." The daughter decided she'd have to be more careful in slipping the homeless some cash.

 Discussion Questions

1. Do you believe that the homeless are really homeless? Or is it a scam?

2. Do you ever help homeless people? How?

3. Have you ever seen homeless people? What were they like? How did they look? Were you afraid of them? Did you need to be afraid?

4. What do your parents think about the homeless problem? What does your church feel about the problem? What is your family or church doing to address and solve the problems of the homeless?

5. If you were asked to develop solutions to the homeless problem, what would your plan be?

6. You and Jesus are out for a walk in a major city and you come upon a group of homeless persons. What does Jesus do?

Possible Topics

Homelessness, helping others, empathy, compassion

Mistaken Identity or Racism?

Alberto is a young Hispanic man who was spending the summer working as an intern at the city hall in Los Angeles. He is an honor student and an outstanding athlete, as well as a leader in his school.

One day while walking home from work toward his apartment, a police car sped up to him and the police jumped out and tackled him. They read him his rights, then arrested him for robbing a nearby liquor store. It wasn't until he was brought to the police station that he was able to prove to them that he was not the person they were looking for.

When the white police officer realized that he had made a mistake, he just shrugged and said, "Oh well, most Chicanos find themselves in trouble with the law at sometime in their life. I guess it just wasn't your turn this time."

Alberto was furious.

 ## Discussion Questions

1. How would you feel if you had been Alberto? What would you have done?

2. Were the police justified in their treatment of Alberto since he seemed to fit the description of the robber? Why or why not? Why do you think they would treat a suspect in such a way?

3. Have you, or someone you know, had a similar experience? What was your reaction? How did it make you feel about yourself?

4. Have you ever made a similar mistake about someone? Have you ever judged someone by their race, ethnic background, looks, economic status or other criteria, rather than as an individual? What were the results of your misjudgment?

5. What can be done to avoid such incidents, or are such misunderstandings inevitable? What can you personally do to try to avoid misunderstanding another person on the basis of external aspects, rather than as an individual?

Possible Topics

Prejudice, stereotyping

Talk Sheets

I love talk sheets. In a practical sense, they bail me out on those rare occasions when I haven't been able to develop a talk for the youth group. Step up to the ol' talk sheet collection and pick a topic. The advantage of talk sheets is that they are self-contained, complete exercises that lend themselves to many applications. They are concise, focused lessons. What an effective way to fill a short lesson time. What a great gift when we are caught long on time, or just short on ideas.

Popeye says, "I yam what's I yam." This is presumed to mean that Popeye can only be what he is and that's what we get. I'm the same way. I teach, share, counsel and minister from who I am. But sometimes it's important to try on someone else's approach. That can be done through a good talk sheet.

For example, as we assembled the talk sheets that follow, I found myself intrigued with the approaches the contributors offered on subjects I have taught dozens of times. Their fresh ideas, their different perspectives, their applications of Scripture were different from my own. It is refreshing to handle a topic with someone else's fresh angle on the subject. Talk sheets are great tools for young leaders to cut their teeth on as well as for more experienced leaders. When encouraging young leaders to step out and lead a meeting on their own, talk sheets provide the inexperienced leader with a balanced means to try out the leadership role with little fear of saying something that is unorthodox. The more experienced youth leader will customize the talk sheet to suit the group's particular personality.

There are many ways to use talk sheets. One of my favorites is to give a talk sheet as a handout to the kids, then ask them the questions on the handout aloud and let them respond as a group. A similar approach is to pass out the handouts, then instruct them to take a few minutes to answer three or four questions. I let them know that the last question, for example, we will be discussing as a group. I often use a talk sheet in tandem with a case study. Use talk sheets however you like. They are good for those spur-of-the-moment talks when you don't have time to think of a good activity or discussion. Learn to use talk sheets by using them in ways that are consistent with who you are. They are that adaptable! Bring yourself and your unique gifts to the talk sheet and make it your own, which will make for a more authentic experience for the kids.

Mark Simone

Mayday! Mayday!

Do you ever feel like the flag on the rope in a tug-of-war battle between God and the devil with your soul as the prize? Are you drowning in a flood, yet thirsty for God? Have you ever felt distant from God even though you're supposed to be a rock-solid Christian? Are you calling out "Mayday!" in the faith department? If so, you can send out a spiritual SOS to God for help!

1. Read Psalm 42. Complete the following rating scale by circling the number that corresponds to the level of your spiritual "appetites":

How much do you relate to...

	Yeah, that's me.			Somewhat like me.			Completely unlike me.		
Panting for streams of water?	10	9	8	7	6	5	4	3	2	1
Thirsty for the living God?	10	9	8	7	6	5	4	3	2	1
Having tears for food?	10	9	8	7	6	5	4	3	2	1
Pouring out your soul?	10	9	8	7	6	5	4	3	2	1
Having waves and breakers sweep over you?	10	9	8	7	6	5	4	3	2	1

2. How close to God did the writer feel as he wrote this psalm?

   a. As far as the east is from the west

   b. So close, and yet so far away

   c. Within arm's length

   d. God is on him like white on rice.

3. Do you think the psalm writer has ever felt close to God?

4. Have you ever felt this way in your relationship with God? When?

What was or is going on in your life that makes you feel that way?

5. How can you put the psalmist's advice into practice in your own life?
   - ❑ Put my hope in God only
   - ❑ Go to church
   - ❑ Go see a waterfall
   - ❑ Talk to a counselor
   - ❑ Praise Him
   - ❑ Other_____

6. Write a prayer that expresses how you feel right now. Use honest language and be open with God.

Not Exempted from Being Tempted

Sometimes we think the Christian life should be free of pain, trouble and temptation. It ain't necessarily so! In fact, Jesus Himself experienced all three. The Bible gives special attention to the fact that Jesus was tempted to sin. And just as the devil gave it his best shot in trying to seduce Jesus, you can expect the same.

Read Matthew 4:1-11, then answer the following:

1. If I had experienced these three particular temptations, I would have...

Temptation #1 (vv. 1-4)

a. Made some "stone bread" to ease my hunger.

b. Told the stones to become prime rib au jus.

c. Resisted putting physical needs above spiritual needs.

Temptation #2 (vv. 5-7)

a. Had some fun at the temple using angels as a bungee cord.

b. Watched with delight the expressions on the priests' faces as I came in for my landing.

c. Avoided doing something spectacular just to get the glory.

Temptation #3 (vv. 8-10)

a. Taken Satan's offer of all the kingdoms for one quick bow.

b. Thought of all the good I could do to make up for only one lapse.

c. Remained focused on my Father in heaven.

2. In falling to any of these temptations, would Jesus have been doing God's will? What *was* God's will for Jesus?

3. Does it surprise you that Jesus, the Son of God, was tempted by the devil? Why or why not?

4. In each instance, what did Jesus do in resisting the devil? (Check all those that apply.)
   - ❑ He quoted Scripture.
   - ❑ He caved in.
   - ❑ He saw through the decei.
   - ❑ He felt he was a victim of peer pressure.
   - ❑ He did not give an inch.
   - ❑ He made the easy choice.

5. How are you tempted in your life? What temptations really get your attention?

6. Is it difficult to resist temptation? Why or why not? What do you do to resist?

Midsummer Blues

Have you said any of the following recently?

"I'm bored!"

"There's nothing to do."

"Oh, I love this episode of *Gilligan's Island*—and I've only seen it 32 times. It's the one where they almost get off the island."

Summer can be fun and exciting—or it can be dull and boring. It can be joyful and Spirit-filled—or a waste of time, a big pain. It all depends on what you do with it. Let's talk about how to break out of our ruts and live life more abundantly as Christ promised.

1. What plans did you make for your summer? List both general plans (e.g., to get a tan) and specific plans (e.g., go to the pool on Mondays and Thursdays) you've made.

2. How's your summer going? Be specific and rate it according to what you expected.

THE AGONY—ECCLESIASTES 1:1-11

3. Is the writer happy and excited about life, or is he depressed and gloomy? How do you know?

4. Have you ever felt like the writer does? What did you do about it?

THE ECSTASY—LUKE 5:1-11.

5. What did Jesus tell Simon Peter to do (see v. 4)?

6. What was Peter's reaction (see v. 5)? What do you think he was expecting?

7. What happened when Peter did what Jesus said (see vv. 6,7)?

8. What effect did this miracle have on Peter (see v. 11)?

9. What lesson is there for you in this story?

10. What are some things you could do for Jesus that would break you out of a dull routine?

It is likely that many of your youth group or church friends are also feeling bored and distracted in midsummer. Ask your youth leaders to help you develop an alternative plan to make this a summer to remember. Use it to help others and show the hurting world around you that Jesus really does care.

"Seek Ye First"

There is always lots of competition for the top spot in people's lives.

Jesus said that the most important thing is to love God "with all your heart and with all your soul and with all your mind." Often, however, He gets crowded out by other things. A famous Christian once said, "Jesus came to be Lord of all, or He will not be Lord at all."

How are you doing with making Jesus the Lord of everything in your life? How can you do better in putting first things first?

Read Deuteronomy 5:7.

1. What kinds of gods would people today be tempted to put before the real God?

Read Matthew 6:19-24.

2. What are ways people store up treasures on earth?

3. How can we store up treasures in heaven?

4. Why does Jesus say you can't have two masters?

Read Matthew 6:33.

5. What are we to seek first?

6. Explain how you personally could do this.

7. Read Matthew 22:37,38. Name the three aspects of your life in which you should put God first. Beside each aspect write one thing you need to do to put God first.

a. _____

b. _____

c. _____

Get together in groups of two or three and in your own words, create a banner or sign that gives a slogan or motto that sums up the message of the Scriptures discussed on these pages. Use any combination of words, pictures or symbols to get the point across. Be prepared to explain your banner to the whole group.

Goin' Bananas!

You can do a lot of fun things with bananas: there's banana splits, banana cream pies-in-the-face, and banana songs such as *Day-O* and *Yes, We Have No Bananas* just to name a few. The term "goin' bananas" means "going to extremes, going overboard, going completely nuts over something." It means to be completely sold out for something.

1. What do you "go bananas" over?

❑ My appearance	❑ Sports	❑ Music
❑ Good grades	❑ Popularity	❑ Friends
❑ Church	❑ Computers	❑ The telephone
❑ Clothing	❑ Myself	❑ Money
❑ God	❑ Food	❑ Girl/Boyfriend

OR MAYBE EVEN...

❑ Pleasing my parents

❑ Pleasing my youth leader (yeah, right!)

2. What is good *and* what is bad about goin' bananas over these things?

Read in Exodus 35:4-9,20; 36:2-7 concerning a nation goin' bananas about giving to God!

3. How did the Israelites show they were goin' bananas over building a sanctuary for God?

4. Can you imagine people in your church having to be *restrained* from giving more?

5. What do you think was going on for this attitude to be so dominant?

Read 2 Samuel 6:9-23 about a king who goes bananas in worship!

6. How did David and the Israelites go bananas over worshiping God?

7. What holds you back from praising God with all of your might like David?

Read Acts 26:19-32 about an apostle who goes bananas for Jesus!

8. What made Festus think Paul had literally gone bananas?

9. What do you think of Paul's witness to Agrippa? Was he courageous? Foolhardy? Crazy?

10. What would it take for you to go bananas in giving to God?

11. What would it take for you to go bananas in worshiping God?

12. What would it take for you to go bananas for Christ?

The Hard Questions

Do you have any deep questions about God, the Bible and Jesus? Many people asked Jesus deep questions. Look up the following verses to read some of the deep questions people asked Jesus:

- How many times should I forgive someone (see Matthew 18:21-35)?

- What must I do to inherit eternal life (see Luke 18:18-20)?
- What is the greatest commandment (see Matthew 22:34-40)?
- When will the end of the world come (see Matthew 24)?
- Are you the One: the Messiah, the promised Savior (see Luke 7:18-23)?

1. Jesus did not get upset with the people who asked Him difficult questions. Questions are natural, but what we do to get the right answers is important. Where have you gone to find answers for your deep questions?

❑ Teachers   ❑ Friends   ❑ Parents

❑ Pastor/counselor   ❑ Television   ❑ Ouija board

❑ The Bible   ❑ Prayer   ❑ Psychic hotline

❑ Teen magazines   ❑ Nowhere   ❑ Others

2. Which of these people/places were helpful? Why?

3. Is there anything wrong with some of these sources? Which ones and why?

4. What would you recommend to a friend struggling with some of these or other important questions?

5. If you had the opportunity to ask God one question right now, what would it be?

We have all heard teachers or pastors tell us that there is no such thing as a stupid question. Remember that God knows our thoughts before we ask. So, don't be afraid to ask God! He loves you, accepts you and loves it when you spend time with Him.

   Ask away! And wait for the response.

Finders Keepers, Losers Weepers

Picture the following situations in your mind:
- Catching a soap bubble
- Holding a snowflake in your hand
- Putting a butterfly in your pocket
- Picking a beautiful flower

1. What will happen to the items in each of the above situations?

Now think about these situations:
- Losing a baby tooth
- Saying good-bye to elementary school
- Graduating from a tricycle to a bicycle
- Realizing your kitten or puppy has become an adult pet

2. What are the results of each of these situations?

What did each of the changes bring?

Matthew 16:25 says, "For whoever wants to save his life will lose it, but whoever loses his life for me will find it."

Here's the point: Attempts to gain or possess something actually bring the loss of that which is sought but when released, something better is gained. For example consider the difference between the first and the second lists above.

There is something mystical in the essence of Jesus' teaching in Matthew 10:39. It speaks not only for the particular point He is making, but also for how it applies in the most personal situations in our lives.

3. What do you think the following statement means?

The greatest Teacher of all time, Jesus Christ, told us that if we try to find our own life, we lose it; if we lose our life for His sake, we find it.

4. What did Paul say in Philippians 3:7 about loss versus gain?

5. What do you need to lose, or change, in order to find your life in Christ? Focus on one thing that you need to change.

It's Not My Fault!

A social worker reports that some teenagers refuse to admit they have any kind of behavior problem, even though they have police records, terrible grades and may not even live with their parents.

Becky once told her social worker, "It's my mom's fault that I hit her. She knew I wanted to watch TV and she said I couldn't."

Zak screams, "I hate this program! I hate the staff! And I hate my dad for sending me to a place like this!"

Lamar yelled, as he was being held down and restrained on the floor, "If he [the victim of his assault] didn't want me to punch and kick him, he shouldn't have talked about my mama that way!"

Each one blames the system, their parents or someone else for the consequences of their behavior, a behavior they often deny. Any thought as to why we sometimes don't want to admit when we have done wrong?

The social worker reported that there seemed to be a pattern in these kids' attitudes: The teens who get into the most trouble are usually the ones who won't acknowledge any responsibility for their choices and actions. Until they stop defending their behavior, they will never change. They never tap into the real life they could have.

At times, we all deny taking responsibility for our actions, especially when the consequences reflect negatively upon us. When was the last time that you made an excuse for your behavior? It is difficult to admit that we have done wrong because we feel ashamed and exposed. James 5:16 says, "Therefore, confess your sins to each other and pray for each other so that you may be healed."

We can only be transformed into the likeness of Christ when we make the choice to walk in truth, no matter how painful that truth may be. Facing the truth of our own mistakes forces us to admit that we are not always able to see ourselves as we would like. But confessing the truth about ourselves, both good and bad, in a safe environment is exactly what we need to help us grow into the people that God created us to be.

Let's Talk About It

1. Think about the times you may have covered up, or denied, the truth about yourself so that others could not see the real you. What were the results of that denial?

2. How did you feel about yourself afterwards?

3. Was the truth eventually revealed? What happened?

4. Why don't we want others to know the real person inside of us?

5. How can you help another person who denies personal responsibility for his or her behavior realize that the prime reason he or she is having so much trouble in life is because of his or her own actions and attitudes?

6. Could the reason that the Bible is avoided by so many people be that it paints an accurate portrait of humanity's true condition and the truth hurts?

Don't Blame Me!

List four things for which society often blames teenagers.

1.

2.

3.

4.

List four valid—real, truthful, legitimate—gripes that society has about today's youth.

1.

2.

3.

4.

TOBY

A friend who works in a psychological agency with emotionally-disturbed kids remembers one boy, Toby, who was extremely unruly, disrespectful and hard to control. Toby was always breaking things in his mom's apartment, getting into school fights and physically abusing his mother. Though he was young, he was more than his petite mom could handle. On several occasions social workers had to intervene with Toby, warning him of the impending doom of being removed from his home by the state and exiled to a setting that would control him. Toby refused to listen. He continued his behavior.

Toby cried as his things were packed and his social services caseworker removed him from his home, yet he still blamed his mother for this new and unfair punishment.

1. Read Jeremiah 7:22-24 and rewrite verses 23 and 24 in your own words.

2. What do these verses say to you?

Like Toby and the nation of Israel, any one of us can be packed up and carried away due to our stubbornness and unwillingness to follow those in authority over us. Share with the group about a time you were stubborn and had to pay a price.

In Ten Years...

Let's look at where you hope to be in ten years. Move beyond today and project into the future.

Try to imagine your life in the next ten years. What will you have achieved?

Where will you be headed? The following questions are guidelines to help you envision your future for the next ten years. Use the second page to record your goals and plans for the next ten years.

Education

How much schooling are you planning on receiving? What kind? College? Trade School? Special training? Armed forces? Apprentice/On the job? What kind of grades do you hope to have?

Job

What kinds of work interest you? What will your career be? How much do you think you'll be making?

Relationships...

With Parents and Siblings

When do you plan on moving out of your parents' home? Will you move completely away or stay close to home? How much time will you spend with family members? What will your family relationships be like? What activities do you see your parents, brothers, sisters and yourself doing together? Will your mom and/or dad baby-sit your children?

With Friends

Who will still be your friends? What new friends do you hope to make? What activities will you be doing with friends? What will you look for in a friend?

With the Opposite Sex

Will you be married? What will your spouse be like? How do you envision your marriage? Will there be children? How many?
Will you be single and in a close relationship with someone? Will you be single and searching for someone? Will you be single and content to stay so?

Physical

What habits do you hope to change? (i.e., smoking, overeating, etc.) What healthy habits will you have developed? What physical activities will you engage in?
How will your personal appearance change? (clothing styles, contact lenses, image makeover, etc.)

Possessions

What will you be buying? What will you fully own? What kinds of things do you hope to have?

Lifestyle

Where will you be living? Describe location (city, country, suburb, East or West coast, mountains, desert, etc.) type of home (apartment, condo, house, cabin, etc.) What kind of life do you want to live: fast-paced, jet setter, quiet, reflective, stay-at-home, travel a lot, etc.?

Spiritual

How do you view your relationship with God over the next ten years? How will your relationship be different than it is now? What will your church life be like? What will your church be like? What kind of ministry would you be involved in?
Will you drop out of church during this time? Why?

Wrap-Up

Put a star on each of the goals you feel you will accomplish.
Put a check mark beside those you feel will be the most difficult to accomplish.
Compare goal sheets with your friends to see your similarities and differences.

My Goals

Personal Data

Name: Today's Date:

Education

Job

Relationships

Family: Friends:

The Opposite Sex:

Physical

Possessions

Lifestyle

Spiritual

Object Lessons

Object lessons are great. In my first youth ministry job after I graduated from seminary, I often gave the children's sermon at our church. I would usually use a fun object lesson to bring home a point the children could understand. I was always amazed that after the service many adults would come up to me and comment on the object lesson. I still remember the time one of the older members in our congregation enthusiastically told me, "It finally makes sense. When you brought out the little duckie and explained the Trinity, it finally made sense!" That day I was reminded that even adults learn best with object lessons even if you use a little duckie to get the point across.

Lately, I've used symbols in object lessons to remind students of an important point of commitment. You may want to try some of the following symbols and see how effective they are for bringing home the point.

Symbols as a Sign of Commitment

Using symbols as a sign of commitment often makes the action more meaningful for students.

The Cross

Last week I passed out special hand-carved pocket crosses to my family and our staff members at National Institute of Youth Ministry. The pocket-sized cross is a tangible reminder of the commitment Christ made to us and of the commitment we have made to serve Him (see Luke 14:27).

A Nail

A common nail can be an outstanding reminder of the sacrificial love of God. In the book of Romans it is very clear that "God demonstrates his own love for us in this: While we were still sinners, Christ died for us" (Romans 5:8).

A Rock

A rock is a great symbol of a commitment or turning point in someone's life just as the Israelites used a stone to commemorate an important covenant or event (see Exodus 24:3-8; Joshua 4:1-9). A rock is also a great reminder that God is our rock and refuge (see Psalm 18:1-3). According to Matthew 7:24-27, the wise person builds his house upon the rock, not the sand.

In my opinion, Mike DeVries is one of the most outstanding and dynamic youth workers in America today. We couldn't think of anyone more qualified to give us great object lessons. All the lessons were presented at his church and resulted in improved communication and learning. We didn't include my little duckie idea. Oh well, you'll just have to find another way to describe the in-depth theological meaning of the Trinity without the use of a duckie. How about a teddy bear?

Jim Burns

Sex and a Blender

Here's a great illustration to drive home the point that God created sex for the marriage relationship. Before the meeting you will need to secure the following items:

- ❑ a blender
- ❑ a small table
- ❑ a glass of water
- ❑ an extension cord
- ❑ a sharp knife
- ❑ a fish (from the grocery store)

Before the meeting begins, place the blender on the small table along with the other items. Use the extension cord to plug in your blender to the nearest electrical outlet.

Before you do this object lesson, talk about God's design for sex to be reserved for the marriage relationship only. Compare sex within marriage to using equipment properly. If you don't use an appliance for what it is designed for, the results could be disastrous.

Hold up the fish. Ask your students, "If you wanted to fillet this fish, what object would you use?" (**Note:** Your students may not know what "fillet" means. Either provide a sample from the grocery store, or

tell them that it means "to cut a thin boneless sideways slice from the fish.") Hold up the knife. Tell your group that this is the proper equipment for filleting the fish, not the blender! Pour the glass of water into the blender, then drop your fish in. Continue to talk about the danger of using improper equipment. Set your blender on puree and let 'er rip! Your point will be made for you.

Conclude the illustration by explaining how getting involved sexually before marriage is like trying to fillet a fish with a blender. The resulting consequences are a mess—not what you want or what God had in mind for the gift of sex.

Possible Topics

Sex and sexuality, dating, purity, chastity

Suggested Scriptures

Genesis 1:26-28; 2:20-25; Matthew 19:4-6; 1 Corinthians 6:18-20; 1 Thessalonians 4:3-7

That Was My Year

Doing a year-end evaluation/challenge talk? Here's a great visual to help your students evaluate their year and set a course for the next year. Secure the following items and have them displayed on a table.

Each item might represent what their year was like. Feel free to add any creative items that you can think of. The following is a list of suggested items and what they represent to get you started:

❏	trophy	Accomplished something big this year
❏	bucket	Bailing yourself out most of the year
❏	toilet	Just a bad year
❏	mirror	God taught you something about yourself
❏	plant food	Grew closer to God
❏	candle	Found Christ this year
❏	junk mail	Useless, a lot of hype, but empty
❏	microwave	Went by fast, really cooking
❏	60x30-inch pair of Levis	A really big year for you
❏	diaper	Kind of stunk

Possible Topics

Goal-setting, evaluation, dreaming big dreams for God

Suggested Scriptures

Nehemiah 1—2; 1 Corinthians 3:10-15

A Box of Potential

This is a great illustration for the potential God sees in each person. Secure two identical boxes. Before the meeting prepare the following items:

- ❑ One gift box filled with paper
- ❑ One gift box filled with paper and include an envelope containing $5
- ❑ Wrap both boxes identically

Display the boxes on a table at the front of the room. Ask for two volunteers to come up to the front of the room. Have one of the volunteers pick one of the boxes to open. Give the other box to the other person. Without opening the boxes, tell everyone that inside one of the boxes is $5 while the other box contains nothing. Ask the group and the volunteers to guess which box contains the $5.

After a minute or two of discussion, have the volunteers open their boxes and the one who finds the five dollars may keep it. Have the volunteers sit down, but leave the boxes and wrappings on the table. Refer to the wrappings as you ask the following questions to introduce your message:

1. Ask the volunteers: Did you believe the box that you selected had the $5 in it? Why?

2. What was the only way to find out which box contained the $5?

Conclude the illustration by talking about how God judges potential and value by what is inside a person rather than what is on the outside. The outside may look the same, but it's what's inside that matters. Stress that the empty box is like a lot of students today, trying to look good on the outside but being empty on the inside.

Possible Topics

Our godly potential, how God sees us

Suggested Scriptures
----
1 Samuel 16:7-13; Psalm 139:1-18,23,24; Ephesians 2:8-10

The White Board

This is an excellent illustration about our need for a Savior. For this illustration, you'll need the following:

- ❑ chalkboard or wall covered with a white sheet or white paper, or a white board
- ❑ clear sheet of plastic large enough to cover the board and the floor directly in front of it (a paint dropcloth is perfect!)
- ❑ masking tape
- ❑ various foods (ketchup, mustard, cooked spinach, honey, egg, jam, syrup, anything colorful and messy)
- ❑ liquid dishwashing soap in a plastic bottle
- ❑ a rag or sponge
- ❑ a pair of rubber gloves

Begin by talking about how we were created in the beginning perfect and sinless (use the chalkboard or white board to represent our condition before the Fall). Tape the plastic dropcloth over the board. As you talk about the Fall of man, start throwing the food items one at a time at the plastic-covered board.

As you throw each food at specific spots on the plastic (try to keep the different spots separate at first), talk about different sins that tempt your students. After you have covered the board with the food, put on the rubber gloves.

As you explain how we humans try to attain salvation by our own works, squirt some dishwashing liquid on the board and attempt to wipe it off. Be sure to make a bigger mess than was previously there.

Then explain how our attempts to attain salvation on our own make our lives messier and messier. Smear everything around to make it even messier.

Now tell them that God took the initiative to help us in our situation by sending Jesus Christ to remove our sin nature, and that if we receive the gift of Christ dying for us, we will be made clean again. Peel off the plastic to reveal the clean board.

Possible Topics
Salvation/decision message, what God did for us through Jesus Christ, the unconditional love of God, redemption

Suggested Scriptures
Psalm 51:1-12; Isaiah 1:18; John 3:16-18; Romans 3:22-24; 5:6-8; 6:23; 10:9,10; Ephesians 2:1-9; Philippians 3:4-9

Fellowship Is Like a Bunch of Charcoal Briquettes

This is an excellent illustration about what fellowship is and why it is essential in our lives as Christians. This would be a great object lesson to use at a picnic, campfire or barbeque and actually light the briquettes so students can see the application. Before the meeting, buy:

- ❑ a bag of charcoal briquettes
- ❑ a box of plastic sandwich bags.
- ❑ You will also need a charcoal grill if you are going to light the briquettes.

To begin the illustration, pour out several charcoal briquettes. (Caution: This will be messy. Pour the briquettes onto a sheet of newspaper if you are not setting them on fire, or into a charcoal grill.)

Say something like, "Fellowship is a lot like this bunch of charcoal briquettes. The thing that makes charcoal work is that when it's lumped together in your barbecue and lit on fire, the briquettes feed off the warmth of the other briquettes. But if you take out one of the briquettes and set it on its own, it will shortly cool off and lose all of its heat. But if you place that lone briquette back in the pile with the other 'on-fire' briquettes, it will once again heat up.

"We're just like that. We need to be in fellowship with other 'on-fire' Christians to keep our own fire alive. Once we take ourselves out of fellowship with others, we begin to 'cool off' in our relationship with Christ. One of the purposes of fellowship is to be around other on-fire Christians who will challenge you to be all that God desires you to be. Don't miss out. Don't cool off. Instead hang out with other Christians who will keep your fire alive for Christ."

At the end of the message give each student a charcoal briquette in a sandwich bag to take home as a reminder of the importance of Christian fellowship.

Possible Topics

Christian fellowship, the Body of Christ, accountability

Suggested Scriptures

Acts 2:42-47; 4:32-35; 1 Corinthians 12:12-26; Galatians 6:2; Ephesians 4:25-32; 5:15-21; Philippians 2:1-4

Sin and the Cross

Looking for a great way to bring home the truth of God's forgiveness? Try this one. Before the meeting you will need to prepare:

- ❑ a cross made of 2x4s—finished size depends on your group's size
- ❑ 3x5-inch index cards—enough for one for each group member
- ❑ pens or pencils
- ❑ a box of nails
- ❑ hammers, several if possible
- ❑ worship music

During the message or Bible study have the cross available for you to refer to while you are speaking. Use the cross as the central visual point of the message or study time.

At the end of the time together, give each student a 3x5-inch index card and a pencil or pen. On the cards have them write down either an area of their lives that they need to surrender to Christ or an area of sin with which they are struggling. Tell them not to sign their names; this will be in the strictest confidence. Supply nails and hammers and have them come up to the cross and physically nail their cards to the cross.

Play some worship music during this time to create a worshipful atmosphere. The sound of worship music, singing and the nailing on the cross are unforgettable.

Possible Topics

Sin, the Cross of Christ, rededication, turning problem areas of your life over to Christ, confession

Suggested Scriptures

Isaiah 53:4-6; Matthew 27:33-54; Mark 8:34-38; 15:22-39; Luke 23:33-47; John 19:17-30; Hebrews 7:26-28; 9:13,14,28; 1 Peter 2:22-25

Being a Ficus for God

Here's a way to challenge your students toward deeper growth in their relationship with God. Before the meeting you'll need to purchase or secure the following items:

- ❑ a small house plant
- ❑ a small pot for the plant
- ❑ plant food (Miracle-Gro or another type of plant food)
- ❑ potting soil
- ❑ glass of water
- ❑ gardening trowel, gloves and apron (for the "dramatic" effect!)

Begin by stating some comparisons between the plant and the Christian life—e.g., we receive Christ and begin our journey as a small seed that begins to blossom into a plant, but to continue in our walk with Christ we need to grow.

Ask group members what it would take for the plant to grow properly. As they discuss some of the things the plant needs to grow, begin repotting the plant in front of the group, explaining each step and the importance of each item or ingredient in the process. Talk about the following items:

- For the plant to grow, we need to take action by caring for it, just as we must with our walk with Christ.
- Each ingredient we use in repotting the plant is essential for its growth, just as there are ingredients that are essential in helping our relationship with Jesus grow, such as reading His Word, prayer, fellowship, worship, spiritual disciplines, etc.

- Just as we may not see the growth in this plant from day to day, over time you see the fruits of growth. So it is with our relationship with God. You may not see growth every day, but over time you'll see growth and its fruit!
- When we begin to "outgrow" our environment (e.g., become complacent and comfortable), we need to be "repotted" (e.g., challenged with a new step of maturity). If we don't move into a new experience, we may become stunted or cease to grow spiritually altogether.

The following outline summarizes the process of growth:
1. SEED IT—begin your relation ship with God.
2. FEED IT—take action by caring for your relationship with God every day.
3. WEED IT—take time to weed out the areas of your life that need to change.

Possible Topics

Spiritual growth/maturity, growing in your relationship with Christ, growth in faith

Suggested Scriptures

1 Corinthians 9:24-25; Philippians 3:12-16; Colossians 1:28; 3:1-17; James 1:2-4

Irish Spring and the Word of God

The next time you talk about applying God's Word to your life, use this object lesson. Purchase ahead of time:

❏ a bar of soap still sealed in the original box or wrapper

Hold up the bar of soap still in its box. Ask the question, "How is God's Word like this bar of soap?" Allow the group to discuss for a few minutes.

Tell the group, "This soap has the power to clean you and remove dirt from your body. Inside this box (or wrapper) is a bar that contains the chemicals needed to clean your body, but as long as the bar is in this box (or wrapper) the chemicals are useless. For me to release the power of the soap to clean my body I need to take the bar out of the box and apply the soap to my body. God's Word is exactly like that. God's Word has the power to transform your life. It has the power to change your life completely, but as long as it sits unopened the power can never be released. God's Word is living and active, and it can change your life, but to release the power you need to apply it. To release the power of God's Word you need to open it up, read it, but most importantly use it in your life. Soap is faithful to accomplish its purpose when properly applied, just as is God's Word."

Possible Topics

Applying God's Word to everyday life, God's Word is life-changing and powerful

Suggested Scriptures

Joshua 1:7,8; Psalm 1; 119:9-16,97,105-112; Proverbs 8:32-35; John 1:1,14; 15:9-11; 17:16,17; Romans 15:4; 2 Timothy 3:14-17; Hebrews 4:12; James 1:22-25; 1 Peter 2:2

What's Your Foundation?

Here's a great way to visually illustrate the story of the wise and foolish builders in Matthew 7:24-27. Before the meeting, borrow or purchase the Jenga game. Before the message or Bible study, set up the Jenga block tower on a flat surface.

Begin by asking your group the question, "What are the shaky foundations people might build their lives on?" Allow the group to respond. After each reply, pull out one block from the stack and replace it on the top of the stack. You can even have students in your group remove a block as they reply to the question. Add a few responses of your own as you continue to pull out blocks from the stack. Eventually the stack will fall over because of the faulty foundation. Continue the message or study by discussing some of the following:

- Why are manmade foundations so shaky?
- What makes a life foundation either strong or weak?
- What needs to happen to a building on an unstable foundation?
- How can an unstable building be corrected?
- How do you need to build a solid, firm foundation on Jesus Christ?
- What tools and equipment do you need to build a strong foundation?

Possible Topics

Building a life on the solid foundation of Christ, spiritual growth, spiritual maturity

Suggested Scriptures

Joshua 1:7-9; Psalm 127:1; Matthew 7:24-27; Luke 6:46-49; John 14:21; 1 Corinthians 3:10-17; Ephesians 2:19-22; 1 Peter 2:4-8

The Words We Speak: Constructive or Destructive?

The next time you are giving a message on the words we speak, use this object lesson as an introduction or discussion starter. Before your meeting, you'll need to secure the following items:

- ❑ a trash can filled with trash (the dirtier and smellier the better)
- ❑ a mirror
- ❑ a gift-wrapped box

Hold up the trash can, then the mirror and finally the gift-wrapped box. As you hold up each item in turn, ask the group, "How does this item represent the words that we speak?"

Allow students time to respond before going on to the next item. When they make their responses, ask them to clarify and give examples or Scriptures that might help them explain their insight.

Either after each item is discussed or after all three have been held up and discussed, be sure to explain the following insights:

The trash can—Sometimes our words are filthy just like this filthy trash can; no one wants to be around us. Sometimes the words that we speak are as useless as garbage in building others up (see Ephesians 4:29; 5:4).

The mirror—Our words reflect what's in our hearts—whether good or bad (see Matthew 12:34-37). Our words can reflect what God thinks about a person. Our words can show someone what is inside of them, even if they don't see it. Our words reflect the levels of our relationships with God.

The gift—Our words can be a gift of encouragement in the lives of others. Just as people treasure certain gifts, our words can be treasures in people's hearts—things they will hold on to when they are discouraged or lonely. Our words can bring a smile to someone's day. Our words of encouragement are a gift of God to others (see Hebrews 10:24,25).

Possible Topics

The power of the words we speak, the tongue

Suggested Scriptures

Proverbs 18:21; Matthew 12:34-37; 15:10,11,18; Luke 6:43-45; Ephesians 4:29; 5:4; Colossians 3:8; Hebrews 3:12,13; 10:24,25; James 1:19-21,26; 3:1-12

I've Changed My Mind

Here's a great way to visually illustrate the idea of garbage in, garbage out and the principle of Philippians 4:8. Before the meeting, you'll need to secure the following items:

- ❑ blender
- ❑ vanilla ice cream
- ❑ chocolate syrup
- ❑ milk
- ❑ large spoon
- ❑ spinach
- ❑ extension cord (if needed)
- ❑ milk
- ❑ small plastic or paper cups
- ❑ ketchup, soy sauce, tabasco sauce, etc.
- ❑ sardines or a fish from the grocery store
- ❑ clam juice
- ❑ any other unpalatable items you can think of

Set up the blender on a flat surface. Begin by talking about the things that we put into our minds and how they affect us. This is an illustration in two parts. For the first part, make a chocolate milk shake using the vanilla ice cream, milk and chocolate syrup. After making the milk shake, pour the shake into a few cups and give to a few students in the group. Talk about the ingredients you've put into the blender to make the milk shake. The delicious ingredients you put into the blender affected what came out of the blender—the chocolate milk shake.

For the second part of the illustration, make another milk shake with the vanilla ice cream, milk, chocolate syrup, and then begin to add the rest of the listed items. As you add the rest of the items, talk about the garbage we sometimes put into our minds—pornography, vulgar music, terrible movies, etc. As you finish with your concoction, ask if anyone would like to have a milk shake now.

Draw the following parallels:

- What you put into your mind affects what comes out.
- What you put into your mind comes out and affects how others view you. (Remember how no one wanted the second batch of milk shakes!)

Discuss Philippians 4:8 and the things with which we need to be filling our minds: whatever is true, noble, right, pure, lovely, admirable, excellent and praiseworthy.

Possible Topics

Purity, integrity, the effects of what we put into our minds

Suggested Scriptures

Proverbs 4:23-27; Romans 12:1,2; Philippians 4:8; Hebrews 4:12; James 1:14,15,21

The Road Signs of Life

Looking for a way to get your students to consider what's going on in their lives and relationships with God? Here's a creative way to get them thinking and talking. Before your meeting construct the following road signs, either on pieces of construction paper or poster board. If possible, get students to help you. Add some creative artwork to make the signs look authentic (or replicas of road signs may be purchased at a learning supply store):

- ❑ Under Construction
- ❑ Detour
- ❑ Winding Road Ahead
- ❑ Dangerous Curve
- ❑ Slippery When Wet
- ❑ Caution

- ❑ Enter at Your Own Risk
- ❑ Rough Road Ahead
- ❑ Speed Limit _____
- ❑ Yield
- ❑ Stop
- ❑ other signs you can think of

Post the road signs around the meeting room. As you begin the message, ask the students to stand under the sign that best represents their lives or relationships with God right now. Don't give any definitions for the signs. Let them select their own meanings for how the signs apply to their lives or relationships with God. Ask several volunteers to explain their choices. This object lesson is a great way to get to know students and how they view themselves and their relationship with God.

Possible Topics

Life direction, self-evaluation, relationship with God

Suggested Scriptures

Psalm 138:8; Proverbs 3:5,6; 14:15; Matthew 7:13; Philippians 1:6

The Candle in the Dark

This is a great object lesson on how we can affect the lives of those around us and how encouragement can multiply God's light in this world. Before the meeting begins, prepare the following:

- ❑ utility candles, enough for every group member to have his or her own
- ❑ small paper plates, with a hole in the middle of each plate
- ❑ matches

As group members arrive, hand a candle and a small paper plate to each person. Have everyone sit in a circle. Instruct them to slip the bottom of their candles into the hole in the middle of the plate.

Say: "We live in a world that is without much hope. Everywhere you turn there seems to be people living without hope. God's Word says that our world is filled with darkness (see Ephesians 4:17-19). Our calling as Christians is to shine out hope in the midst of our dark world. One way that we can shine out hope to our world is through encouraging one another."

Read Hebrews 10:24,25 and say: "Tonight, we're going to live out this verse by shining out the light and hope of encouragement to one another."

Light your candle, then turn out the lights. Ask everyone to stand up and stay in the circle. Select one person in the group, walk to that person and tell him or her one encouraging thing while lighting his or her candle. After you have lighted the first candle, that person in turn will do the same to another person in the room. Continue until everyone in the room has their candles lighted. When this is accomplished, comment about how one light passed along to another eventually illuminated the whole room. You might want to end this time of encouragement by singing a praise song or with a time of prayer. Have students blow out their candles and turn on the lights before continuing.

Review Hebrews 10:24,25, then read John 13:34,35. Spend some time talking about the power of encouragement in our lives as well as bringing light into a dark world. Say: "In a real sense, when we encourage those around us, we are being a light in our darkened world. We are showing that we are followers of God."

Have students keep their (unlit) candles as a reminder to be a light in their world through the power of encouragement.

A word of caution: You should check with fire and safety codes before you do this activity inside a building.

Possible Topics

Encouragement, building up the Body of Christ, speaking encouragement to others, the power of the tongue

Suggested Scriptures

Proverbs 18:21; Matthew 5:14-16; 12:34-37; John 13:34,35; Ephesians 4:29-32; 5:8,9; Hebrews 10:24,25

Discussion Starters

Educators often refer to *the teachable moment*. It is that special experience in a learning setting when the learners are primed and begging for words of wisdom to spill from your mouth. It is that occasion when the students are so into the program or topic that they would rather sit and listen to you than take a trip to the mall or a movie. In youth ministry it does not often happen, but it is wonderful when it does.

Over the years I have found that the teachable moment can be manufactured, allowing for more opportunities to really grab the kids' attention and share with them. It is controlled and directed by you, the leader, but it appears to the kids to be something that just happened. Discussion starters are a valuable means to bring the teaching moment into being.

A discussion starter is a brief statement that is sometimes weighty, sometimes nonjudgmental, sometimes silly, sometimes poignant and always interesting enough to promote youth to circle up the wagons and talk. It's that question or comment that somehow capsulizes what is going on and turns it into a relevant discussion.

Recently I noticed a prominent teenage leader in our group give the international sign of displeasure to some friends as she left the church parking lot. I was shocked and very surprised, so I went outside and asked the kids what was up. Without batting an eyelash, they told me it was the new gesture of affectionate joking. They related it to any ethnic group who uses the slang terms of their nationality in descriptive conversation among themselves. It was a teaching moment.

I responded, "What if your mom or

Pastor Dave saw that? What might they think?" And we were off. The spontaneous conversation soon evolved into a discussion on appropriate public and private behavior of believers. After all, we are supposed to be ambassadors for Christ.

Try some discussion starters on those way-too-long bus rides, or while sipping a soda, or when you're just with the kids. Learn to manufacture wonderful teaching moments by using discussion starters.

Progressive Decision–Making Discussion Starters

The following situations call for the group members to make decisions as a jury would. These true stories are revealed to the group in steps. Each step is a bit more complicated and may find some of the kids changing their answers as the story progresses. Some details in the stories were changed to protect identities.

Important: Whenever possible, ask students to back up their decisions or their reasoning with Scripture.

The Dying Prisoner

Part One

In Ohio, a convicted alcoholic was sentenced to four years in prison for habitually driving under the influence of alcohol. After serving his first year, he was diagnosed with a liver disease that would soon kill him. Through his lawyer he has petitioned the court to grant him a release so that he might die with his family near him and not all by himself in prison.

Talk about the facts as you have heard them. Would you let him out or not? Defend your answer. Are there any Scripture verses that back up your thoughts?

Now vote: Release him or keep him in jail? Why?

Part Two

You should also know that this man was convicted on *nine* counts of driving under the influence of alcohol. The courts can only speculate how many times he was DUI (Driving Under the Influence) without being caught. He is 34 years old, is married and has two kids. The man has also been arrested for breaking into other people's cars to get in out of the weather when he could not locate his own car. It was also reported that he had stolen cars on various occasions to get home.

Consider this new information, vote again and defend your vote.

Part Three

The man's request for release is being supported by his wife and family. She wants him to die at home surrounded by those who love him, and she adamantly claims that he has hurt no one through his alcoholism. She maintains that he has been sober for a solid year and does not believe he will fall into drinking again. His children want him home in time for what may be their final Christmas together. The doctors maintain that this man will not recover and will probably die within a year.

Discuss, debate, apply Scripture and vote. Consider the statement that he has hurt no one through his alcohol usage. Is that true? Should he be released or kept in jail?

Part Four

Finally, just prior to entering jail the man risked his life to save another person's life. Details were not given about his deed, except to say that it truly was an act of heroism. Does this factor change your vote?

Conclude the discussion by letting the group mull through the difficult aspects of this case. Help them to see that life is rarely as cut and dry as we think. Above all, help them to see that Jesus loves this man, even though he is in jail.

The Abusive Potluck

Part One

A group that is not associated with First Church asked if it could hold its meeting at the church. Permission was given and the group assembled for a potluck dinner. The table-tops were lined with delicious food and the participants were anxious to dig in. In fact, one fellow was so hungry that he did just that—he dug into a bowl of salad with his hand, scooping a handful of salad onto his plate. Across the table in the other line, a woman took offense at this man's behavior and told him off in front of everyone.

The pastor overseeing this gathering was alerted to the problem when the police entered the fellowship room. They had been called by the woman who claimed that the man had struck her. The police were there to take the man into custody.

By the facts as we know them, you decide if this scenario is appropriate to the outcome: the police being called and the man being arrested. Remember to back up your reasoning with Scripture whenever possible.

Part Two

It seems that the man did smack the woman. While she was telling him off, he simply gave her hand a smack.

Does this fact change your previous decision?

Part Three

The man says that the woman who had brought the salad was moving through the line with him. She told the man that she had forgotten to bring any type of serving utensil and with a laugh she reached into her salad with her hand and put her serving on her plate. She apparently told the man that if he wanted salad, he'd just have to follow her lead and grab some. So he did. That was when the other woman across the table saw him and began the confrontation.

Does this change your thinking? Now we know that the man was not the first to put his hand into the salad, and that the salad's owner encouraged him to reach in. Of course, we still have the fact that the man slapped his accuser's hand. How do these new facts affect your opinion?

Part Four

The final detail is that another witness to this ghastly, heinous crime told the police that the woman who had been smacked had not mentioned that she had struck the man

first. When he put his hand into the salad bowl, she reached over as she was telling him off, and slapped his hand a number of times while it was still in the salad bowl. In fact, this witness says that the man did not smack her as much as hit her hand away to get her to quit hitting him.

Now it looks like this bizarre situation is a battle. She slapped his hand several times; he hit her hand away. Then in anger she called the police, requesting they arrest the man.

You decide—what is right and what is wrong here? Who's at fault and why? If you were the police, how would you handle this situation? Finally, how could this whole mess have been avoided?

Another vein to consider is what kind of publicity this brings the church. The church was providing space for a group that had no meeting place, yet the church gets this strange story printed in the local paper's police report. What kind of testimony of Christ does this present to the rest of the community? Should the church give groups like this the boot? Or is this an acceptable risk?

The Teenage Murderer

Part One

Troy is very good looking, a promising all-county football star and the son of a very well-liked family. He is quiet, but very intelligent and well regarded by his friends and teachers. In his first year of playing football, he proved to be a natural athlete and received widespread news coverage as he made great play after play. Already the college scouts are talking to him, and he's only a sophomore.

Very early one morning, Troy's parents called Stan, the church youth pastor, and asked him to come to their home immediately. Troy was being arrested for the murder of his girlfriend and he had admitted to killing her.

Given these facts, discuss how this might unfold. Troy has admitted he is guilty so how should he be treated? Consider his age as you determine his fate.

Part Two

Visiting Troy in jail, Stan found out that Troy had broken up with his girlfriend Amber weeks before. She had become possessive and dependent upon him. She was disturbing Troy's concentration. His athletic ability was going to be his ticket to college. Troy flipped out when Amber continued to call him at all hours of the night. His parents were very angry at the 3 A.M. phone calls which awakened the whole household. Troy was told to take care of the problem. Lacking good coping skills, Troy was in anguish over Amber's continued calls. He was not sleeping and obviously struggling internally with the pressure. He didn't know what to do to solve this conflict.

How do these new facts play into your thinking? Is he now any less guilty? Are his parents somewhat responsible? And what about Amber? We can see that murder was totally inappropriate, but does her stalking Troy lessen his guilt? Remember to use Scripture to back up your reasoning whenever possible.

Part Three

The newspapers have covered this case as though Troy were destined for athletic sainthood. Many of the writers continually mentioned Troy's incredible skill as an athlete and the waste of a promising career. As the weeks passed and the case dragged on, this sad loss became a strong aspect of the case. Amber's ceaseless bothering of Troy got lots of coverage as well. The reporters seemed to excuse Troy of responsibility for the crime.

At a meeting of Troy's youth group, one young woman quietly asked a pointed question, "What about all that Amber has lost?" Silently, each one considered this question.

What do you think of the facts? Is great athletic ability sufficient reason to lament the waste of a life? Have the papers lost perspective? And what about Amber?

Part Four

Troy got 30 years in a maximum security prison for his crime. He will be nearly 50 years old when he gets out. Compassionately, his church has continued to support him while he is in prison. Numerous people write to him and remember him at Christmas and his birthday. He has become a Christian in prison and is the chaplain's assistant. He knows God's Word very well and works tirelessly to introduce other inmates to Christ.

The youth pastor still keeps in touch, too. Recently Troy asked Stan if the church would allow him to return upon his release. Stan automatically assumes so, but during the long drive home, he decides that he needs to bring this up to the church's governing body. At the next meeting of the church council, Stan asks the leaders Troy's question. In dead silence each member thinks of how they will respond on that day when Troy is released, having paid his debt to society and returning to his church home.

What would you say to Troy? Could you worship God sitting next to him? What would be the ramifications on the church membership? Should Troy disappear and live in another community? If you knew Amber, could you forgive Troy?

The Jail Visit

Part One

During the weekly visit to the jail, youth pastor Al found himself in a very fulfilling conversation with a new inmate, Stephen. Al's rule was to never ask the prisoners what their crimes had been. If they offered this information, fine, but Al felt asking was inappropriately nosy.

In the weeks that followed, Stephen became Al's favorite prisoner. Not only was he open to the gospel, he was bright, witty and a solid thinker. It was refreshing to Al to share his faith with someone so clearly seeking.

Then Stephen ruined everything by telling Al that he was in jail for the crime that Al perhaps hated the most. Stephen had been arrested for rape.

What would you say to a rapist? How would you feel if you were Al? What about Stephen? Does he have a right to become a Christian? What would you do?

Part Two

Sensing Al's discomfort, Stephen closed up and shortly the two said good-bye. Al was very troubled by Stephen's crime, and he could not believe that his new friend was such a scumbag. Rape seemed to him a total violation to all that God and society held holy. It was such a life-damaging transgression. In his previous work in a crisis center, Al had talked to many women and girls who struggled with the devastating feelings caused by rape. Nothing could be more harmful to a woman's feelings of self-worth, trust or security. Al simply could not deal with this new revelation and he decided to never visit Stephen again.

Is Al acting in a Christian manner? Is he giving Stephen a fair shake? Keep in mind that rape is Al's personal bottom-line sin and he has had lots of experience in counseling women and girls who were raped. Do we all have a bottom line that helps us know our personal limitations? How might Al put closure on this?

Part Three

Al is unable to live with his decision and in a couple of weeks he visits Stephen again. The talk is not flowing as in past visits and Stephen knows that Al is struggling. Stephen asks Al for permission to share his story. Al agrees and listens.

Stephen tells Al that there is no excuse for the crimes he committed. He makes no claim to be a poor misunderstood victim of society. In fact he, too, hates himself for the rapes he committed. Al shudders and Stephen responds that, yes, he has raped more than once. He raped three women in one week.

Stephen tells Al that not long ago he had been happily married to the dearest woman ever. Unexpectedly, she died. In his grief he found help from his family. His mother was especially understanding and he spent quite a lot of time with her. Suddenly, she also died. Stephen thought he was going to die as well. The two women he loved the most had abruptly been taken from him with no warning. In time, he healed somewhat and was able to face the world.

Shortly after, he met a new woman and fell in love. Talk had turned to marriage and Stephen was amazed that he thought he just might be willing to tie the knot once again. Soon after they became engaged, she was killed in a car accident. Al was dumbfounded by this unbelievable story.

Stephen began believing that women were trying to escape from him. He became insanely angry. In his madness he raped a college woman, then another and one more—all within a week's time. His insane behavior left an open trail for the police to follow and he was soon arrested.

You decide: Do these facts change the way you feel? Talk about how life must have seemed to Stephen. How should Al feel, knowing all of this? If you were a jury, how would you deliberate at Stephen's trial? And isn't Al on trial in a sense? Should a Christian be more accepting and forgiving of those who commit terrible crimes?

Part Four

Stephen asked for no special treatment. He only wanted the whole story to be considered in court. He had not tried to avoid justice in any way. He was willing to face the consequences of his behavior. Only then could he live with his crimes.

However, Stephen also wanted a relationship with Jesus Christ. Al had convinced him that Jesus could forgive him and restore him. Stephen believed that jail time with the company of Christ would be beneficial to his rehabilitation.

Close out this case by deciding what justice really is. Is it "an eye for an eye" as the Old Testament says? Or is it forgiveness in Christ? Perhaps it is a combination of the two. You decide.

Two Strikes Against Missions

Part One

With the new youth worker at Victory Community Church, a seminary intern, came a wealth of building skills. It seemed that Sam, the second-year seminarian, came from a family that owned a contracting company.

The high school group at Victory had never been on a work camp before. As Sam described his experiences in helping the needy by offering them competent repairs to their homes as a sign of Christ's love, the whole youth group became excited about new ways they could reach out.

The obvious problem was that not one kid in the group had any building experience. Sam assured them all—guys and girls—that they could all do far more than they ever believed. And he would love to teach them how. For the first time, missions looked like it could be very interesting.

Have you ever gone on a work camp? Share your experience with the group. If not, would that be a cool way to help others? How might the recipients feel having strangers travel from a distance to fix up their homes? How might you feel if you were helping them? What is keeping your group from going on a missions work camp?

Part Two

Sam thought that the best plan would be for the group to visit a local building project which was constructing affordable housing for poor families right in their town. He called the project director and discovered that there was going to be a house raising in two weeks and the organization would love it if Sam brought the youth group over to help.

On a warm Saturday morning, 17 teenagers stepped out of church vans and walked onto a lot that was filled with people, lumber, tools, equipment and the concrete block foundation of what would soon be a frame house. Sam led his gang in a prayer of dedication and they joined the other workers.

Throughout the day, the group members from Victory did nothing but pick up litter and lumber scraps. Not one excited, ready-to-work teenager was asked to swing a hammer or drive in one nail. At day's end, the group reentered their vans with heavy, disappointed hearts.

Were these teenagers expecting too much from their work day? Would you have been disappointed? It could be said that cleaning up trash was as important to the project as

building walls and securing beams. Shouldn't the group from Victory feel good about their contributions to the work?

Part Three

Sam felt bad about the building project and knew he had to help the group rebound from the disappointment. He sensed they needed a strong mission experience to reignite the fire that was so evident before they were delegated to litter detail.

Asking around, Sam found an inner-city soup kitchen that needed helpers at their regular Sunday meal. Excitedly, Sam shared his prior soup kitchen experiences with the group. Again, they caught his enthusiasm, and the following Sunday a group of 21 teenagers walked through the doors of an inner-city church and descended to its basement soup kitchen.

The kids loved it! They prepared the food, served meals, cleaned up and played with children. Some sang choruses to those eating and many chatted with those being served. Sam felt good about bringing the kids.

As the meal came to its conclusion, one of the young women came to Sam, obviously terrified, and told him that a man had tried to coax her upstairs for sexual favors. She was shaken by his language and descriptions of sexual activity. Moments later, one of the young men from his group came to seek comfort. While asking for another cup of coffee, an elderly man had verbally attacked this young man with a foul racial slur. Because safety could not be assured, Sam gathered his group, loaded them into the vans and left the soup kitchen.

As the group headed home in shocked silence, Sam wondered what he could do to restore a sense of mission to these young people who had now experienced two significant strikes against their missionary zeal.

Discuss how you feel about these incidents. What should Sam do? What should he tell his students? What could they do to rectify the problems? How can the two experiences—one sexual and one racial—be explained? Why do such things sometimes happen when helping others? Did Sam do the right thing in removing the kids from the soup kitchen? Why or why not?

Part Four

Sam realized he had a looming problem and sought God for direction. With two strikes against them, the youth group was understandably resistant to considering any further summer missions programs or experiences.

At the next youth meeting he opened up to the kids and asked them what they, as a group, should do in response to these horrible experiences. Gently, he confronted the teenagers with the belief that bad experiences do not exempt the follower of Jesus from

continuing to help others, citing various examples in Scripture. Sam asked for ideas or suggestions.

One young woman, Teresa, spoke up and said that before they think of new projects, they better look at what did not work in the last two. She suggested that in learning from the bad, they might be able to invent a missions project that made sense to the group.

Out of two disastrous experiences, these teenagers put together a plan for their own soup kitchen to be housed in the gym of an inner-city church with which their church had a yoked relationship. They developed solid security safeguards. They listed appropriate norms for behavior. They even figured out the first year's menu.

From the ashes of bad experiences came a successful food assistance program that meets the ministry needs of the teenagers and the physical needs of the homeless and poor. Soon after, the same group of teenagers decided to organize their own work camp adventures. At these work camps, all participants equally share the duties of sawing and hammering, as well as cleaning up litter.

Could these mission programs have come into being without the unfortunate experiences of the first two strikeouts? Defend your answer. Was it possible that these teenagers might have developed a philosophy that it is too risky or too menial to help others? How closely involved with work camps and other service projects should teenagers be? Are today's teenagers responsible, capable and concerned enough to take on major work camp or food assistance projects? What about your group? How are you serving others?

Short Discussion Starters

The following are shorter talk initiators that present a single brief story or idea that will likely divide the group in opinion. These stories can be used as warm-ups for bigger topics, as introductions to Bible studies or as brief stand-alone lessons.

Students love to talk and with these discussion stimulators, they can wrestle with what they perceive as reality and discover how others may perceive it differently. Luring the group into a discussion is a great way of providing a service to the teenagers that they are unaware of—the opportunity to face a serious dilemma before they must face it in real life.

The Abused Donation

An elderly woman gave the youth group a shoe box full of old, used plastic dolls from the 1970s. She believed that the kids would like them and asked us to give them out. Looking into the box the youth pastor discovered that it was filled with the old Troll dolls—the naked plastic dolls with long, wispy hair dyed in bright colors. She was psyched because the Trolls were making a strong comeback.

She gave the dolls as goofy prizes after the game time at the next youth meeting. The girls were really excited. The boys were somewhat skeptical, but played along. The leader told the students how these prizes had come to the group and mentioned the name of the woman who had donated them.

A little while later, one young woman came to the youth leader very upset and disquieted. She told the leader that the boys were dismembering the dolls and she felt it was a waste and disrespectful to the spirit of the donation. The boys maintained that these were their prizes to do with as they wished.

Discuss both points of view. Was it okay for the boys to dismember the dolls or was their behavior disrespectful? Was this a legitimate complaint? When you receive a gift, do you feel free to do with it exactly as you wish? Why or why not?

The Frightened Youth Leader

In Maggie's first year of youth ministry, she had made incredible strides at First Church. She had revitalized the youth group, nearly quadrupling the number of kids attending. Her work was still in the early stages, but she was off to a good start.

One day at a picnic by the beach some of the kids tried to pick up Maggie, who was still in her street clothes, and throw her into the water. Struggling, and definitely not laughing, Maggie protested. The youth ignored her and began pulling her into the lake. Suddenly, Maggie began shrieking and threatened to quit her job if she was thrown in. All laughter ceased and the kids awkwardly put her down. Maggie continued to yell at them, completely losing it. The day was ruined.

Discuss Maggie's reaction. Was she being fair? Was she acting like a responsible leader? What do you think was going on in Maggie's mind? Could there have been a legitimate reason for her desperately angry reaction? Did Maggie have the right to protest? Do you think she's clueless about the nature of youth ministry? How do you think the youth group members feel about her threatening to quit? How do you think the group could have ministered to Maggie after the event? What should Maggie do now? What really bothers you about this true story?

Joint Custody

After their divorce, Mr. and Mrs. Kramer had agreed upon joint custody of their three kids. Both parents lived within the school district so school attendance was not affected by the arrangement—the kids would live with their dad the first and third weeks of the month and with their mom the second and fourth weeks. However, what was problematic was dividing time between the two churches that their parents attended. This was especially difficult for Lennie, who was very active in the youth group of Fellowship Christian Church. It was the church that his family had always attended as he was growing up and his dad still attended. More importantly, it was Lennie's church.

Yet, Lennie's mom insisted that he visit the youth group of her new church, Grace Chapel, during the weeks he spent under her care. The group was okay, but Lennie was a member of the worship band and a student discipleship leader at his church. He simply did not know how to be active in both groups. In his depression, he's ready to give up and quit both groups.

What do you think about Lennie's parents' arrangement for the kids? Is it a good set-up? Is Lennie being rigid and unfair? Should he try to accept both groups? Why or why not? Suggest a solution. What should Lennie tell his parents? How would you react if this were your life? Is anything in your life similar to this story?

The Scam Artist?

Carol was approached by a scruffy-looking man. Although his appearance made her uncomfortable, she tried to listen to the man as he told her of his hard luck and asked for a few bucks. Her leaning was to give it to him, but her friend Sean whispered to her that this guy was probably a big-time drug user and that he would only go buy whatever drugs he could with the money.

The desperate man seemed sincere as he told Carol that he was very hungry and would only use the money for food. He had to eat. Noticing Carol's Bible, he reminded her that Jesus helped the poor. Carol glanced at her Bible and then into the eyes of the man. Sean tugged at her arm. In a flash of movement, Carol took five dollars from her pocket and thrust it into the man's hands. She asked him not to buy drugs with it and to please use it for food. The man's eyes at first showed surprise, and then despair. He became fidgety, hurriedly thanked her, then asked Carol to pray for him as he quickly walked down the street.

Discuss where you think this man went with Carol's money. Did he buy drugs or food? What would you have done if you were Carol? What about Sean? Was he being fair? Do you think the man was manipulating Carol unfairly by taking note of her Bible? The world is filled with sad stories and hurting people. What is the best way for us to be supportive of them while not feeding their problems?

Wanting to Make It

Anthony was really bumming. He had long paid his dues to be considered for student government at his high school. His list of credentials was quite impressive: principal's office aide, president of the jazz and art clubs, honor-roll member, the marching band treasurer and general good guy. He really liked school and saw his time and energy investment as being worth the accomplishment of his goal to be the senior class president.

And now after a tough campaign, the vote indicated that Shawna was the new senior class president. He had lost. The disappointment was heightened by the fact that Shawna had been elected totally because of her popularity. She was cute, very personable and very *un*interested in the politics of the school. She had run on a whim to receive more attention and had thoroughly trounced Anthony. Perhaps more disconcerting—Shawna had no idea what the issues and challenges of school leadership were. She would likely do nothing to enhance the overall climate of the school.

Losing the election made Anthony wonder if God really knew what He was doing. He had firmly believed that God was moving him along a path of leadership that would benefit not only the student body, but also the Body of Christ. And now what was happening?

Discuss Anthony's election loss. How would he feel? How would you feel if the same thing happened to you? Why would God lead someone to try to reach a goal, and then allow such a disappointing result? Could it be because that person has made mistakes, or has hidden sin, or simply a matter of the world's influence on the vote of others?

What would you tell Anthony if you were his friend? Discuss the plight of not feeling God's support in the tasks we undertake for His glory. Talk about God's power and knowledge, and why God might be holding Anthony back from this leadership experience. Could God be showing Anthony something in this that will help him as a leader later? What might those things be?

What kind of leader will Shawna turn out to be? Is the popular vote reliable for good leadership choices? Have you voted for the most popular student when you knew that another candidate would probably be a better leader? Explain why you voted as you did.

Stealing Sheep?

After many years of doing nothing together, the youth workers and pastors in a major city decided to band together to promote a combined concert and mission program. Although the pastors came from different branches of Christianity, their differences had been placed on a back burner to make certain that the event would honor the unity of the Body of Christ and bring about an event that would glorify Him and affect the lives of the youth of the community. For the first time ever, the teenagers of this community were able to see that many students at their schools were also believers. It was an exciting time for the leaders and students alike.

Just before the event, the students from Faith Church began mingling with many of the other teenagers and began passing out small packets of reading material. Sara, a leader in her youth group at Grace Fellowship, was given a packet. The guy who handed it to her asked her not to read it until she returned home. He was so cute that Sara could not resist, so she went to the ladies' room and opened the packet. She was shocked to see that it was an invitation to visit Faith Church. Listed were the special youth events, Bible study schedules, church worship times and a coupon to join the kids from Faith Church at a midnight movie party at the mall. The youth group had rented the theater for a private invitation-only showing of a major movie that all of the kids were talking about.

Sara was shocked. The youth group of Faith Church was using the joint youth group event to steal sheep from the other youth groups. With sadness, Sara went in search of her youth pastor.

Discuss this true story. Are the students and leaders of Faith Church being honorable or dishonorable? Are they playing fair or is this in bad taste? Have you ever seen a similar situation in your area? What happened?

What is wrong with this evangelism tactic? Since the Bible says we should reach out to others, is Faith Church doing the right thing? How would you feel if such an effort by another church suddenly cleaned out your youth group? What if some of the students who left to attend the other church accepted the Lord or became more disciplined Christians as a result of the switch? Do churches have an obligation to respect other ministries and not try to grow by "stealing sheep"?

That's Why We Hired You!

As the new youth leader, Connie was anxious to get to work. In her first months, she tried to spend equal time in getting to know the kids and in planning for the future of the youth program. She had so many ideas and there were so many opportunities. The only thing her program lacked was adult helpers. With enthusiasm to share her new ministry, she set out to recruit advisors.

The congregation was not large, but it was amply gifted. Over the next few Sundays, Connie surveyed her church family and began making note of likely prospects for youth ministry advisors. With nearly a dozen excellent possibilities, she began making visits and calls, asking them to join her in ministering to youth.

At first those who said no had good reasons—they were newly married, or pregnant, or had a time conflict, or were taking college classes—so Connie was not too discouraged. However, when she reached the end of her list, she began to sense an underlying resistance.

She finally spoke frankly to Adam, who was a well respected, energetic young man with a strong and active faith. When Connie approached him, she was shocked by his reply: "Look Connie, some of the other people you've asked called me to warn me that you were going to be asking me to help you in youth ministry. The bottom line is that's what we hired you to do. So don't bother asking."

Discuss how Connie must have felt hearing Adam's statement. What would you have said? What would Jesus have said? How should church ministry, on all levels, be approached and accomplished? Was Connie trying to put her workload off on others? Is ministry the responsibility of the pastor alone, or is it to be shared?

Flirting, Harassing or Loving?

The youth group was very close for many reasons. The youth pastor, Seth, had invested nearly a decade among the kids at Valley Church. As a result, he was able to watch "his kids" grow from junior high into the college-age group. He and the present and former members of the youth group shared lots of history, experiences and growth in Christ to knit them together in devoted relationships.

At a program of shared ministry with other churches that brought together a number of Christian youth groups, Seth was called into a serious and private meeting of the leaders. Thinking it was a planning meeting for the remainder of the programs, Seth was devastated to discover that his ministry peers had determined that his behavior was inappropriate. In questioning what they were talking about, one pastor said that Seth's actions had brought complaints about his behavior that the other leaders had also witnessed and agreed on. Asking for specifics, Seth was told that hugging and putting his arm around his kids was not to be tolerated. One even noted that Seth had kissed one of the girls after she won a competitive event. His ministry colleagues believed that he was either flirting with the young women in his group, or possibly sexually harassing them. Shocked, Seth was unable to defend his actions. For the remainder of the program, Seth sat in the back of the room near tears.

Was Seth behaving in an inappropriate manner with the kids from his youth group? What if he did the same actions with kids from other groups? How far is too far when showing affection to another Christian? What can Seth learn from this? Has a youth leader ever made you feel uncomfortable? What, if anything, did you do about it?

Movie Mistakes

The outdoor event was rained out, so Ann, the church youth worker, decided on a last-minute change to take the kids to a bargain movie matinee. Looking over the movie choices, she told the kids not to attend any movie that would be inappropriate. "PG-13 and below," she said. With four acceptable movies out of the eight available at the Cineplex, she felt that the kids could be trusted to choose one that was not controversial.

The next day Mrs. Davis called and in an angry voice told Ann how disappointed she was that Ann had allowed her daughter to attend an R-rated movie. The mother had just returned from viewing the movie herself and quoted numerous conversations that were filled with sexual innuendoes and awful language. While there were not actual scenes of these behaviors, the discussions were too descriptive.

Ann knew that Mrs. Davis's daughter had purchased a ticket for one of the PG-13 movies. It seemed that she and her friends had left the movie they intended to watch and sneaked into another. Now, Ann had to pay the price by answering to this irate parent.

What should Ann say to Mrs. Davis? Where do Ann's responsibilities end and the teenagers' begin? Is the parent right to be disappointed in Ann's decision? How can this problem be solved? What can be done to avoid a similar situation? How can such an incident be destructive to the people involved? To the youth group? How can this be turned into a learning situation?

Movie Mistakes II, the Sequel

This time we find a different spin on the above scenario. LaKeshai decided to take her church group of mostly African-American youth to see a current movie that investigated inner-city gang behavior. The movie looked at relationships, risks and the opportunities that gang members face on a daily basis. In their own community, gang activity was just beginning to be evident among teenagers and LaKeshai feared that ignoring the reality would seem to be a message that gang life is okay. Wanting to be proactive, she let all the parents and students know what to expect so they could responsibly decide who should or should not attend.

During the week following the movie, LaKeshai was bombarded with phone calls from parents who found the whole subject distasteful. They believed that LaKeshai was introducing "gang thinking," as they called it, to their teenagers who probably would never think of joining a gang. A few parents noted that their sons and daughters would no longer be attending youth group as long as LaKeshai was leading.

Did LaKeshai make a bad decision by taking the group to see this movie? Could she have avoided this conflict in some way? Are the parents being fair? If you were a parent, what would you tell LaKeshai? If you were LaKeshai, what would you tell the parents? Does ignoring a problem help the problem go away? Why or why not? What might Jesus do?

Truth or Lies?

Tony and Ellen were in love. Plain and simple. Their friends and family teased them by saying their love was just "puppy love" because they were only in high school. They would reply with good humor that puppy love was good for the two of them because they *were* puppies.

Nearly everyone appreciated the maturity of Ellen and Tony's relationship. Teachers, friends, even their pastor mentioned that the relationship was based on trust, commitment and respect. They were not inappropriately affectionate in public, and they tried to center their dating relationship in Christ. Most agreed it was a dating relationship to hold up as an example to others.

However, Tony's non-Christian parents were not so supportive of his time with Ellen. They constantly tried to control his time, and they often said unkind things about Ellen. It saddened Tony, but he prevailed in good spirit.

The crushing blow came when Tony's dad said that Tony could no longer go to church youth group with Ellen. "Why," he demanded of his son, "don't you and your girlfriend go out like other kids? You only go to church—no movies, no late-night partying, nothing exciting or fun." Then it hit Tony. His father was embarrassed and perhaps convicted by Tony's moral and pure lifestyle. He wanted his son to go out boozing, not praying, and he was afraid Tony was wasting the best time of his life.

Tony realized that if he played by his dad's standards, then his dad had no problems with him dating Ellen. So Tony began lying, telling his dad that he and Ellen had gone to a wild party or to the movies or to the park. The result was no more complaints from Dad.

The lying was hurting Tony, but it seemed to be the only way for him to see Ellen. She was not aware of his lies and thought everything was going well. Finally under strong conviction, Tony suggested to Ellen that they drive through the places he was telling his parents they were visiting on the way to church youth group. The request was so strange that Ellen probed Tony for his reasons. Tony then told her of his father's disappointment and how he was trying to appease his dad by lying about going to undesirable activities and places. He rationalized that if they drove through the places he claimed they were going to that it wasn't really a lie.

What do you think of Tony's father's demand? What do you think about Tony's solution? Should Tony have conformed to his father's wishes or is it okay for him to lie for a good reason? What might happen if Tony's parents find out he is lying? How would you react if you were Ellen? What should Ellen and Tony do? Should Tony continue to lie so they can stay together? Should they break up? What are some possible solutions?

And You Thought You Had a Bad Day!

Here are several true stories about bad days with some unusual consequences. These stories can extract good discussions from your group concerning God's care of us.

Where is God in the midst of our bad days? Read one or more of the following stories. What was God's part in each incident? Was He responsible for the tragedy? What was the responsibility of the unfortunate person in each occurrence?

A fierce gust of wind blew 45-year-old Vittorio Luise's car into a river near Naples, Italy in 1983. He managed to break a window, climb out and swim to shore—where a tree blew over and killed him.

Mike Stewart, 31, of Dallas was filming a movie in 1983 on the dangers of low-level bridges when the truck he was standing on passed under a low-level bridge, killing him.

Walter Hallas, a 26-year-old store clerk in Leeds, England was so afraid of dentists that in 1979 he asked a fellow worker to try to cure his toothache by punching him in the jaw. The punch caused Hallas to fall down and hit his head. He died as a result of a fractured skull.

Surprised while burgling a house in Antwerp, Belgium, a thief fled out the back door, clambered over a nine-foot wall, dropped down and found himself in the city prison.

George Schwartz, owner of a factory in Providence, Rhode Island, narrowly escaped death in 1987 when an explosion flattened his factory except for one wall. After treatment for minor injuries, he returned to the scene to search for files. The remaining wall collapsed on him and killed him.

A man hit by a car in New York in 1977 got up uninjured, but laid back down in front of the car when a bystander told him to pretend he was hurt so he could collect insurance money. The car rolled forward and crushed him to death.

In a classic case of one thing leading to another, seven men aged eighteen to twenty-nine received jail sentences of three to four years in Kingston-on-Thames, England, in 1979 after a fight that started when one of the men threw a french fry at another while they stood waiting for a train.

In 1976 a twenty-two-year-old Irishman, Bob Finnegan, was crossing busy Fall Road in Belfast when he was struck by a taxi and flung over its roof. The taxi drove away and as Finnegan lay stunned in the road, another car ran into him, rolling him into the gutter. It too drove on. As a knot of gawkers gathered to examine the magnetic Irishman, a delivery van plowed through the crowd, leaving in its wake three injured bystanders and an even more battered Bob Finnegan. When a fourth vehicle came along, the crowd wisely scattered and only one person was hit—Bob Finnegan. In the space of two minutes, Finnegan suffered a fractured skull, broken pelvis, broken leg and other assorted injuries. Hospital officials said he would recover.

While motorcycling through the Hungarian countryside, Cristo Falatti approached the railroad tracks just as the crossing gates were coming down. While he sat idling, he was joined by a farmer with a goat that the farmer tethered to the crossing gate. A few moments later a horse and cart drew up behind Falatti, followed in short order by a man in a sports car. When the train roared through the crossing, the horse startled and bit Falatti on the arm. Not a man to be trifled with, Falatti responded by punching the horse in the head. In consequence the horse's owner jumped down from his cart and began scuffling with the motorcyclist.

Hitting on the novel idea that he could end his wife's incessant nagging by giving her a good scare, Hungarian Jake Fen built an elaborate harness to make it look as if he had hanged himself. When his wife came home and saw him, she fainted. Hearing a disturbance, a neighbor came over and finding what she thought were two corpses, seized the opportunity to loot the place. As she was leaving the room with her arms laden, the outraged and suspended Mr. Fen kicked her stoutly in the backside. This so surprised the lady that she dropped dead of a heart attack. Happily, Mr. Fen was acquitted of manslaughter, and he and his wife were reconciled.

Two West German motorists had an all-too-literal-head-on collision in heavy fog near the small town of Guertersloh. Each was guiding his car at a snail's pace near the center of the road. At the moment of impact their heads were both out of the windows when they smacked together. Both men were hospitalized with severe head injuries. Their cars weren't scratched.

The Fire Plan

Each time Mr. Higgins read of a house fire in the newspaper, he mentioned to his wife how important it was to develop and practice a fire escape plan for them and their children. Mrs. Higgins always agreed, noting that they had so much to lose and it was easy to be prepared. Occasionally the two would draw out on paper or discuss the best ways to escape the house if a fire occurred. However, they never actually tried out the plan. The family moved quite a lot with Mr. Higgins's work and a new fire plan was necessary with each new home.

Sadly, the Higgins family only truly got serious about a fire plan after their house and possessions were completely lost in a devastating fire. They barely escaped with their lives and Mr. Higgins was severely burned while trying to find his children and help them escape. Although the family survived, the life-changing injuries to Mr. Higgins and the trauma of this horrifying experience have dramatically affected the whole family.

How could the Higgins family have been better prepared? What is wrong with an untried plan? How does such a story apply to our Christian lives and spiritual growth?

The Witch at Bible Study

The founding leader of a witchcraft coven began visiting a church Bible study. First, she sat in the back and respectfully listened. Then she sat closer and began asking questions. Lately, she has been more involved and has asked for prayer for some family needs at the closing prayer circle. All the while she is still leading her witchcraft group that continues to grow and practice satanic rituals which the Bible clearly condemns.

As the Bible study leader, how would you confront the situation? How would you react if you found out one of the members of your Bible study group was a witch, or involved in some other type of occultic practice? What might you say to this young woman if she came to you? How would you determine if the witch was trying to influence the Bible study or if she was truly seeking God? How does the following verse apply to this situation: "Greater is He who is in you than he who is in the world" (1 John 4:4, *NASB*)?

Storybook Ideas: Dr. Seuss and Other Stories

Good children's stories are always a hit. Though written to capture the imagination of children everywhere, these stories can often be used to teach deeper spiritual truths. On the following pages are a few samples of children's stories that you can use.

The Sneetches & Other Stories
by Dr. Seuss (Theodor Geisel)

This is a great tale about what it takes to really be valuable. Use *The Sneetches* to help students evaluate their self-images, what to value, where they gain significance and how far they will go in their search for value and significance. (Random House Books for Young Readers: New York, 1966)

Possible Topics

Seeing the value of ourselves and others, self-image, significance

Suggested Scriptures

1 Samuel 16:7; Psalm 139:1-18; Ephesians 2:10

Did I Ever Tell You How Lucky You Are?
by Dr. Seuss (Theodor Geisel)

No matter who you are or what you've been through, thankfulness is a *choice* of attitude. This story illustrates thankfulness as only Dr. Seuss can. Students will be impacted by how fortunate they really are. (Random House Books for Young Readers: New York, 1973)

Possible Topics

An attitude of thankfulness, gratitude

Suggested Scriptures

Psalm 100:1-5; 107:1; Habakkuk 3:18; Luke 17:11-19; Ephesians 5:19,20; Philippians 4:6,7; Colossians 3:15-17; 1 Thessalonians 5:16,18

Yertle the Turtle & Other Stories
by Dr. Seuss (Theodor Geisel)

This book contains three incredible stories. *Yertle the Turtle* focuses on the issue of status and what we sometimes do to others to obtain it. *Gertrude McFuzz* focuses on comparing ourselves to one another, coming up short, what we will do to be "better than" and finally realizing that being ourselves isn't that bad after all. *The Big Brag* looks at comparisons and the foolishness of boasting about oneself and pridefulness. ((Random House Books for Young Readers: New York, 1966)

Possible Topics

Looking out for number one, humility, comparison, servanthood, boasting, pride

Suggested Scriptures

Jeremiah 9:23,24; Matthew 20:25-28; 23:11,12; 1 Corinthians 1:31; Galatians 6:14; Philippians 2:1-11; James 4:6

It's Not Easy Being a Bunny
by Marilyn Sadler

This story takes a look at a bunny who decides one day that he doesn't like being a bunny. So he takes off in search of what he really wants to be, only to find out that the best thing he can be is what he was created to be. A great story that illustrates the value that God places in each of us, and points out our search for significance. (Beginner Books, A Division of Random House, Inc.: New York, 1983)

Possible Topics

The value we have in Christ, significance

Suggested Scriptures

Psalm 139:1-18; Jeremiah 29:11-14; Ephesians 2:10

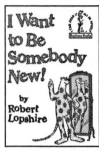

I Want To Be Somebody New
by Robert Lopshire

This book is great for teaching about comparing ourselves to others and trying to be something we are not. The character decides to explore what it would be like to be somebody new and ultimately finds out it's best to just be himself. (Beginner Books, A Division of Random House, Inc.: New York, 1986)

Possible Topics

Self-image, how God values us, significance

Suggested Scriptures

Psalm 139:1-18; Jeremiah 29:11-14; Galatians 6:4; Ephesians 2:10

The Giving Tree
by Shel Silverstein

An incredibly popular story about a relationship between a tree and the boy she loves. It's a great illustration of giving of yourself completely for another person regardless of the cost and circumstances. (HarperCollins Children's Books: New York, 1964)

Possible Topics

Giving to others, putting love into action

Suggested Scriptures

John 13:12-17,34,35; 1 John 3:16-18; 4:7-12

The Tale of Three Trees
by Angela Elwell Hunt

A traditional folktale that's a wonderful illustration of God using the ordinary in extraordinary ways. Also great for a message about sacrifice, God's sovereignty and giving your dreams to God. (Lion Publishing, A Division of Chariot Family Publishing: Colorado Springs, Colo., 1989)

Possible Topics

God using the ordinary for the extraordinary, sacrifice, giving yourself fully to God

Suggested Scriptures

Isaiah 64:8; Jeremiah 18:1-6; Romans 9:21; 2 Corinthians 4:7; 2 Timothy 2:20

The Runaway Bunny
by Margaret Wise Brown

A story of a bunny who decides to run away from its mother, yet no matter where the bunny chooses to run, the mother is right there with open arms and love. A great illustration about the type of love that our heavenly Father has for each of us. No matter where we run, He is always there. (Harper Torchbooks: New York, 1977)

Possible Topic

God's unconditional love

Suggested Scriptures

Luke 15:11-31; John 3:16,17; Romans 8:38,39

The Song of the King
by Max Lucado

A wonderful story about three knights and their quest for the hand of the king's daughter. Each knight is put to the test of going through the dark forest. Two emerge defeated; only one is successful. The point of this story will have your students talking for weeks. (Crossway Books, A Division of Good News Publishers: Wheaton, Ill.,1995; 1-800-635-7993)

Possible Topics

Clinging to God, knowing His voice, courage, victory

Suggested Scripture

Joshua 1:5-9; John 10:1-18;
1 Corinthians 16:13

The Velveteen Rabbit
by Margery Williams

The classic children's story about what it means to be real. When the Velveteen Rabbit wants to know what being "real" means, the Skin Horse is the authority. This creative story is an excellent way to introduce and discuss the issues of being real and transparent, and of demonstrating true love. (Tor Books, A Division of Tom Doherty Associates, Inc. & St. Martins Press: New York, 1995)

Possible Topics

Being real/transparent, giving and receiving love

Suggested Scriptures

1 John 3:16-18; 4:7-12

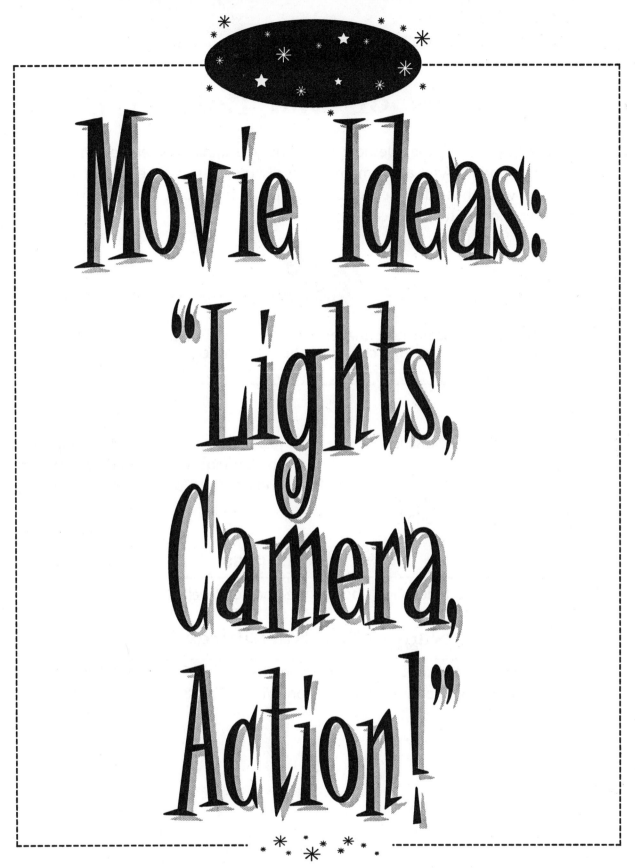

Movie Ideas: "Lights, Camera, Action!"

A great way to illustrate an idea or theme is by using video clips from movies. Movie and television clips are powerful ways to bring the Word of God into focus for this media-raised generation.[1] On the following pages are a few ideas to get you started:

Raiders of the Lost Ark

To introduce this clip, ask the question: "What do you think of when you think about the end of the world?" After a few moments of discussion, say: "There are a lot of different ideas of what the end of the world will be like. Some people think it will look a lot like this." (Paramount Studios, Lucasfilms Ltd., 1981)

Cue the video to begin near the end of the movie where the Ark of the Covenant is opened. Stop the clip when the Ark is closed.

After the clip is finished, discuss the following questions:

1. What does God's Word have to say about the end of the world?

2. Read Matthew 24:42-44. What are some things we need to do to stay alert and be ready for the Lord's return?

Possible Topics

End times, God's power, the book of Revelation

Suggested Scriptures

Matthew 24:42-44, Mark 13:3-37; 1 Corinthians 13:12; 1 Thessalonians 4:15—5:11; 2 Peter 3:3-14; 1 John 3:2,3; Revelation 4:1-11; 21:1-8; 22:7,12-14,20

Indiana Jones and the Last Crusade

Introduce the video segment by saying: "Faith is more than just a belief, it's stepping out in action. What you are about to see is an excellent example of what faith is all about. Faith is not just believing in something, it means taking action on what you believe." (Paramount Studios, Lucasfilms Ltd., 1989)

Cue the video to begin at the part where Indiana Jones is about to make his step of faith across the chasm to get to the chamber of the Holy Grail. Stop the clip when he successfully crosses the chasm.

After the video segment, designate a line down the center of the room. Designate one side of the room the "Agree" side and the other the "Disagree" side. Read the following statements and have your group members move to the side of the line that represents their opinion. Have some members of each group discuss their opinions.

- Agree/Disagree: Seeing is believing.

- Agree/Disagree: How you live your life reveals what you believe.

- Agree/Disagree: True faith is a blind leap into the unknown.

Discuss the following questions:

1. When have you had to step out in faith?

2. Why is it tough to step out in faith?

3. What are some things that keep us from acting on our faith?

4. What are some situations in your life right now in which God is asking you to "live by faith, not by sight" (2 Corinthians 5:7)?

Possible Topics

Faith, demonstrating your faith, seeking God's will

Suggested Scriptures

Mark 9:17-24; Luke 1:26-38,45-56; Romans 4:18-21; 2 Corinthians 5:7; Philippians 4:13; 2 Timothy 1:12; Hebrews 11; James 2:14-26

Field of Dreams

This classic movie deals with the dreams we have for the future as well as dreams about the past.

Introduce the segment by saying: "God wants to use us in radical ways to change our world, but it begins with a dream of making an impact for Him. God is in the business of making incredible dreams for Him become a reality." (Universal City Studios Inc., 1989)

Cue the clip to begin where Kevin Costner's character asks his father to play a game of catch and stop the clip at the end of the movie.

After the video segment, ask the following questions:

1. If you could be involved in making an impact in our world in any way, what would you want to do?

2. What keeps us from dreaming big dreams for God?

3. What can we do as a youth group to make an impact in our world in a tangible way?

Possible Topic

Dreaming the impossible for God

Suggested Scriptures

Nehemiah 1—2; Joel 2:28; Acts 2:17,18; Philippians 4:13

Mr. Holland's Opus

This is a phenomenal movie about the impact one person can have on those around him.

Introduce the clip by saying: "You may be the only Jesus somebody will ever know. As Christians we have an impact on those around us—positively or negatively. Sometimes we wonder if we can make an impact on those around us. The answer is *Yes!* God wants to use you in the lives of those around you." (Hollywood Pictures, 1995)

Cue the clip to begin where Mr. Holland enters the gym for the surprise celebration held to honor his work. If time allows, show the clip until the end of the movie. If time is limited, the most important part is the speech made by one of his successful former students at the celebration.

After showing the video, ask the following questions:

1. What type of impact do you want to have on those around you? How do you want to view them?

2. What do you think keeps many Christians from having a positive impact on those around them?

3. Who in your life do you want to have an impact on? What will you do about it?

4. Who has had an impact on you? Why?

Possible Topic

Making an impact in the lives of others

Suggested Scriptures

Matthew 10:42; 18:19,20; Luke 6:27-36; 10:30-37; Acts 2:38-41; 3:2-10; 4:36; 14:21,22; 1 Corinthians 13:4-8; Galatians 1:11—2:2; 6:2-6; Philippians 1:3-6; 1 Thessalonians 2:8-13; 1 Timothy 1:15,16

School Ties

In this movie the main character is entering a prestigious prep school and encounters more than just academics. Being a Jew, he discovers the cruel reality of racism. This movie chronicles his struggle with who he is, what he wants to be and how others see him. (Paramount Pictures, 1993)

Cue the clip to begin with the confrontation when his roommate discovers that he's trying to hide the fact that he is Jewish. It's a great scene to use when talking about racism, acceptance and being who God created you to be.

Discuss the following questions:

1. Have you experienced being treated like an outcast? Describe your feelings about the prejudice of others.

2. What do you think God thinks about the issue of prejudice against a certain racial or ethnic group? What are some Scriptures you can find that speak out about racism or prejudice?

3. If you could do something to solve the issues of prejudice and racism, what would you do about it?

Possible Topics

Prejudice, racism, self-acceptance

Suggested Scriptures

Matthew 22:37,38; Luke 10:25-37; John 10:16; 17:9-11,20-23; Romans 12:3; 1 Corinthians 12:12,13; Galatians 3:26-28; Ephesians 2:14,15; 2 Peter 1:5-9

Quiz Show

This movie is based on the true story of the rigging of a TV game show in the 1950s. The main character is sucked into the deception by the producers of the "Quiz Show." The plot thickens when the show is investigated for fraud and the main character is caught in the center of it all. This is a great movie to use for discussing deception, temptation, honesty, integrity and the cost of integrity. (Hollywood Pictures, 1994)

Cue the video to begin when the main character is reading his statement before the grand jury near the end of the movie. Stop it when he finishes the statement.

Discuss the following:

1. What are your thoughts about the main character? Is he a person of integrity or not? Why did he do it?

2. Why is it difficult to be a person of integrity?

3. What are some of the costs of being a person of integrity?

4. What can you do to exhibit more integrity in your life?

Possible Topics

Honesty, integrity, deception, temptation

Suggested Scriptures

Genesis 20:1-7; 39—41; 1 Kings 9:4-9; Psalm 15; 25:1-21;
Proverbs 10:9; 11:3; 12:17; 29:10; 1 Timothy 4:12; Titus 2:6-8

Dead Poets Society

This movie deals with a group of friends attending a prestigious prep school. Their life takes a dramatic turn when their literature class is taught by a new teacher (Robin Williams). This movie is filled with usable clips that will strike a cord with young people and their desire to make a significant impact on the world. The following is just one of the possibilities: (Touchstone Pictures, 1988)

Cue the video to begin when one of the students returns home and tells his parents that he's going to pursue his gifts and become an actor, only to find them opposed to his dreams for the future. The incident ends with the student taking his own life.

Discuss the following:

1. What are some things that keep us from "seizing the day" and living out our dreams?

2. What are some of the personal expectations you feel are laid on you and other teenagers today?

3. If you could have any dream in your life become a reality, what would it be?

4. What vision do you carry in your mind and heart about making an impact on the world for Jesus Christ?

Possible Topics
Youth culture, expectations, dreams for the future, suicide

Suggested Scriptures
Ezekiel 22:30; Joel 2:28,29; Matthew 5:1-9; 25:31-46; Acts 2:17,18; 1 Timothy 4:12

Molder of Dreams

This Focus on the Family production is an excellent tool, especially for training and encouraging volunteers in youth ministry. It looks into the thoughts and dreams of Guy Doud, who was selected teacher of the year several years ago. It has many memorable quotes and sections that will challenge volunteers with the incredible impact they have on the lives of students. It will challenge them to be more intentional in their ministry, as well as encourage them in what they are already doing in the lives of the kids they work with. (Focus on the Family, 1990)

Show the complete video.

After viewing the video, discuss the following:

1. Who are some of the people who have had an impact on your life? How did they influence you?

2. Who are the people that you can have an impact on? What are you doing to have a positive influence on them?

3. If you were to die today, what would you want written on your tombstone or said about you at your funeral?

4. What character qualities would you like to see developed in the people that you are pouring your life into?

Possible Topics

Making an impact on those around you, encouraging youth workers, teachers and parents to "hang in there" with young people

Suggested Scriptures

1 Thessalonians 2:7,8

Ali Baba Bunny

This Warner Brothers cartoon starring Bugs Bunny and Daffy Duck is an excellent tool to challenge students about materialism, greed and giving. Daffy Duck finds a hidden treasure and tries to horde it all for himself. The results are hilarious and will keep your kids talking for weeks about the effects of materialism. The classic line from the cartoon is "Mine, mine, all mine!" (*Warner Bros. Cartoons Golden Jubilee Bugs Bunny's Wacky Adventures,* Warner Bros. Inc., 1985)

Show the whole cartoon.

Discuss the following:

1. How have you seen the attitude of "mine, mine, all mine" lived out in our world today? In the lives of teenagers today?

2. What makes us a world that is so focused on things?

3. This cartoon shows that greed brings about a downfall. What happens in our lives when we're ruled by greed and materialism?

4. What do you think is God's desire for us concerning the things we have?

Possible Topics
Materialism, greed, giving, stewardship

Suggested Scriptures
Matthew 6:2-4,19-21,24,33; 2 Corinthians 9:6-8; 1 Timothy 6:9-10; Hebrews 13:5

Other Video Ideas

Dr. Seuss Books on Video

Many of the classic Dr. Seuss books that can be used as discussion starters are also available on video if you prefer to use that medium instead. *How the Grinch Stole Christmas* is just one example of a Dr. Seuss book that is available in video form. Many other children's books previously mentioned in the "Storybook Ideas: Dr. Seuss and Other Stories" section are also available on video.

TV Sitcoms

Sitcoms can give you some incredible looks into the world as portrayed by Hollywood. Popular sitcoms that your students are currently watching can be used to show the heart and desire of young people: discussions on sexuality, friendship and other relevant issues.

Afternoon/Late Night Talk Shows

Talk show interviews can give your group some added food for thought on a variety of different issues. Check your TV guide for upcoming topics and people being interviewed. Videotape appropriate shows and look for usable material for discussion starters, lessons or Bible studies.

Newscasts

Usually the first two to five minutes of a newscast can give you enough material for a discussion starter or Bible study. Look for current events that kids are talking about as possible material. The news clips can be used for a study on our world, society, the nature of man, God's sovereignty or to discuss the age-old question, "If God were in control, why does this kind of thing happen?"

Lights! Camera! Action!
Making Your Own Video Discussion Starters

Here's a creative way to get your students to discuss their own opinions as they talk about the issues that matter the most to them.

Before a message or study, interview some of your students on the issue. Ask them their thoughts, what they do about it, what advice they would give. Show the video interview as a discussion starter for the message of the study.

Some great issues for using this method include: sexuality, drinking, stress, worry, thankfulness, parents, friends, prayer, making healthy choices and decisions.

Use your imagination and creativity in using this medium with different issues and questions.

Note:
1. Although the Federal Copyright Law, Title 17 of the U.S. Code prohibits the use of rented video footage outside the renter's home, the "Fair Use Doctrine" permits portions of copyrighted works to be legally reproduced for purposes of criticism, comment, news reporting, classroom teaching, scholarship and research. More information on these laws can be found in *The Church Guide to Copyright Law*, Richard Hammer, Christian Ministry Resources; P.O. Box 2301, Matthews, NC, 28106 (704-841-8066).

Contributors' Submissions

Dead Poets Society
Field of Dreams
Indiana Jones and the Last Crusade
Molder of Dreams
Mr. Holland's Opus
Quiz Show
Raiders of the Lost Ark
School Ties
Other Video Ideas

TOM PATTERSON
Is He the Only Way?
The Mission Trip
What Is Reality?

MARK SIMONE
The Abused Donation
The Abusive Potluck
The Accident
Assault on a Soda Machine
Being the Minority
By Chance, Not by Choice
The Campus Confrontation
Can Dish It Out, but Can't Take It
Delinquents or Outcasts?
The Dying Prisoner
The Fire Plan
Flirting, Harassing or Loving?
The Frightened Youth Leader
I Am a Christian
The Invisible Homeless
The Jail Visit
Joint Custody
The Missing Mugs
Movie Mistakes
Movie Mistakes II, the Sequel
The New Christian
Pizza Night Divorce
The Scam Artist?
Stealing Sheep?

The Teenage Murderer
That's Why We Hired You!
Truth or Lies?
Two Strikes Against Missions
Wanting to Make It
What's in a Name?
The Witch at Bible Study

JONATHAN TRAUX
Goin' Bananas!
The Hard Questions
Mayday! Mayday!
Midsummer Blues
Not Exempted from Being Tempted
"Seek Ye First"

DAIV WHALEY
Don't Blame Me!
Finders Keepers, Losers Weepers
It's Not My Fault!

COLLECTED FROM THE INTERNET
And You Thought You Had a Bad Day!

Topical Index

Scripture Reference Index

Old Testament

Genesis

1:26-28	57
2:20-25	57
20:1-7	109
39—41	109

Exodus

24:3-8	56
35:4-9,20	41
36:2-7	41

Deuteronomy

5:7	39

Joshua

1:5-9	102
1:7,8	64
1:7-9	65
4:1-9	56

1 Samuel

16:7	98
16:7-13	59

2 Samuel

6:9-23	42

1 Kings

9:4-9	109

Nehemiah

1—2	58, 106

Psalm

1	64
15	109
18:1-3	56
25:1-21	109
42	33
51:1-12	60
55	24
100:1-5	98
107:1	98
119:9-16,97,105-112	64
127:1	65
138:8	68
139:1-18	98, 99, 100
139:1-18,23,24	59

Proverbs

3:5,6	68

New Testament

Give Junior Highers Meat to Chew!

Junior High Builders

Each reproducible manual has 13 Bible studies with tons of games, activities and clip art for your handouts.

Christian Basics
ISBN 08307.16963

The Life and Times of Jesus Christ
ISBN 08307.16971

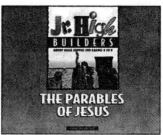

The Parables of Jesus
ISBN 08307.16998

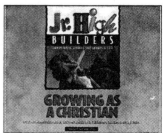

Growing as a Christian
ISBN 08307.17005

Christian Relationships
ISBN 08307.17013

Symbols of Christ
ISBN 08307.17021

The Power of God
ISBN 08307.17048

Faith in Action
ISBN 08307.17056

Lifestyles of the Not-So-Famous from the Bible
ISBN 08307.17099

Great Old Testament Leaders
ISBN 08307.17072

Great Truths from Ephesians
ISBN 08307.17080

Peace, Love and Truth
ISBN 08307.17064

Ask for these resources at your local Christian bookstore.

Gospel Light

Take High Schoolers Deep Into God's Word

YouthBuilders Group Bible Studies

These high-involvement, discussion-oriented, Bible-centered studies work together to give you a comprehensive program, seeing your young people through their high school years–and beyond. From respected youth worker Jim Burns.

Give Your Youth *The Word On:*

The Basics of Christianity
ISBN 08307.16440

Being a Leader, Serving Others & Sharing Your Faith
ISBN 08307.16459

Finding and Using Your Spiritual Gifts
ISBN 08307.17897

Helping Friends in Crisis
ISBN 08307.16467

The Life of Jesus
ISBN 08307.16475

The Sermon on the Mount
ISBN 08307.17234

Prayer and the Devotional Life
ISBN 08307.16432

Sex, Drugs & Rock 'N' Roll
ISBN 08307.16424

Spiritual Warfare
ISBN 08307.17242

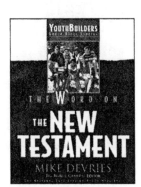

The New Testament
ISBN 08307.17250

The Old Testament
ISBN 08307.17269

Family
ISBN 08307.17277

Ask for these resources at your local Christian bookstore. **Gospel Light**

Youth Ministry Resources from Gospel Light

YouthBuilders Group Bible Studies

The Word on:

Sex, Drugs and Rock 'N' Roll
ISBN 08307.16424

Prayer and the Devotional Life
ISBN 08307.16432

Basics of Christianity
ISBN 08307.16440

Being a Leader, Serving Others & Sharing Your Faith
ISBN 08307.16459

Helping Friends in Crisis
ISBN 08307.16467

The Life of Jesus
ISBN 08307.16475

Finding and Using Your Spiritual Gifts
ISBN 08307.17897

The Sermon on the Mount
ISBN 08307.17234

Spiritual Warfare
ISBN 08307.17242

The New Testament
ISBN 08307.17250

The Old Testament
ISBN 08307.17269

Family

Jr. High Builders

Christian Basics
ISBN 08307.16963

The Life and Times of Jesus Christ
ISBN 08307.16971

The Parables of Jesus
ISBN 08307.16998

Growing as a Christian
ISBN 08307.17005

Christian Relationships
ISBN 08307.17013

Symbols of Christ
ISBN 08307.17021

The Power of God
ISBN 08307.17048

Faith in Action
ISBN 08307.17056

Peace, Love and Truth
ISBN 08307.17064

Great Old Testament Leaders
ISBN 08307.17072

Great Truths from Ephesians
ISBN 08307.17080

Lifestyles of the Not-So-Famous from the Bible
ISBN 08307.17099

Generation Next
George Barna

Find out how to reach today's teens during this critical period in their lives. Help them cut through confusion and find honest answers to the questions they have.

Hardcover • ISBN 08307.17870

Micro Messages
Tom Finley and Rick Bundschuh

30 quick, complete one-page messages, each featuring accompanying evangelism tracts with an attitude.

Manual • ISBN 08307.15789

My Family, My Friends, My Life

This powerful 12-session study helps youth understand God's plan for relationships, starting with their own families. Includes reproducible student pages and "Parent Page" to take lessons into the home.

Manual • ISBN 08307.16947

The Youthworker's Book of Case Studies
Jim Burns

Fifty-two true stories with discussion questions to add interest to any Bible study.

Manual • ISBN 08307.15827

Show Youth Their Identity in Christ

Stomping Out the Darkness
Neil T. Anderson and Dave Park

Here is the powerful message from Victory over the Darkness written especially for young people that provides youth with keys to their identity, worth, and acceptance as children of God.

Paperback • ISBN 08307.16408
Study Guide • ISBN 08307.17455

Busting Free
Neil T. Anderson and Dave Park

This youth group study helps young people find biblical solutions to the personal and spiritual wounds that cripple their self-esteem and confuse their identity.

Manual • ISBN 08307.16653
Video Seminar • UPC 607135.000808

Outrageous Object Lessons
E. G. VonTrutzschler

Do you teach using mousetraps, birds and seeds? Jesus and Jeremiah often used object lessons and you can too! Teaching tools—from the simple to the outrageous—present Bible principles in vibrant, new ways.

Manual • ISBN 08307.14960

Super Clip Art for Youth Workers on Disk
Tom Finley

The latest high-quality clip art to supercharge flyers and newsletters. Includes disks, instructions and book.

Windows Disks • SPCN 25116.06607
Macintosh Disks • SPCN 25116.06593
Win/Mac CD-ROM • UPC 607135.002604

Gospel Light

Ask for these resources at your local Christian bookstore